Unpunished

Unpunished

D.D.K.

authorHOUSE®

AuthorHouse™
1663 Liberty Drive
Bloomington, IN 47403
www.authorhouse.com
Phone: 1-800-839-8640

Published by AuthorHouse   11/08/2012

ISBN: 978-1-4772-8096-6 (sc)
ISBN: 978-1-4772-8095-9 (hc)
ISBN: 978-1-4772-8097-3 (e)

Library of Congress Control Number: 2012919443

Edited by Karin Kirkland

Sources for the articles:
Cayman Free Press
Cayman Net News

Special Thanks to My Gals:

My "Sista" Karin
Armelle
Angie
Cheralyn
Debbie
Pauline
Rosalie
Shannon
Tammy
Taryn

and my kidlets!

Prologue / Introduction

Donna was driving along the winding country road taking in the view of the river together with the beautiful gold, amber and scarlet leaves that were lightly falling from the trees. She never tired of the drive home, since it was always so breathtaking in any of the four seasons. She stopped at the end of the lane to get her mail as she had done so many times before. There were a lot of the usual fliers but one letter with no return address instantly caught her attention. The handwriting was shaky, as though written with a vibrating pen. It must be from her elderly mother she thought as she excitedly opened the letter, not waiting to drive home first. Donna felt a twisting knot in her stomach as the pictures fell out into a pile on her lap. She recognized where she had once been in the photos, only now she was viciously and intricately cut out. He was back again

It all began to come back, the humiliating history, all of the emotional, physical and traumatic episodes, which had made her life a living hell. So *many* instances in the past that went . . . *unpunished.*

Chapter 1

*D*onna's mother Mary was a tough, hard woman. At the same time she had gentleness about her, always wanting to rescue people, particularly children. She was beautiful with platinum blonde hair and turquoise blue eyes. Mary was a small framed woman. Donna's father Alan was Mary's third marriage. He was a handsome, well-built man with dark thick hair and stunning green eyes. He worked as a mason and did various construction work. Donna had a half-sister from her mom's first marriage and two half-brothers from her second. Her mother had raised Donna alone with her oldest son as support. She gave Donna most of what she needed. She worked long hours as a hairstylist and her feet were always swollen. Donna was always terrified as a child of losing her mother. She didn't think she could live without her. She wanted her mother to love her, as *much* as she loved her mother.

Her father had run away from the Ukraine during the war. He never spoke about it until later in life, while in a drunken stupor. He would serve in three different armies, somehow managing to survive the grip of death. He had left a family of four daughters and one son behind. Donna's mother and her father's son Peter wrote to each

1

other for many years. Peter knew it was a matter of survival that caused their father to run and his letters were heartwarming. Donna believed it was the underlying cause of her father's alcoholism, "medicine" was what he called it, every morning and every night, it numbed the pain.

During the war, her father and his brother were lined up with many other soldiers in front of a huge pit, which was to become their graves. The men fell backwards into the death pits from the bullets that tore through them. Her father and his brother were spared from death by falling into the pits without being shot. They lay buried beneath the bloody corpses of the men they had fought alongside. After five hours and the sound of silence, they cautiously peeked out from below the bodies in the pit. He was relieved to see that his brother was alive as well. They made a pact to meet in England. Her father ran one way and his brother in the other direction. Eventually they both made their way to England; however they never saw each other again. Her father had apparently fathered a child there. He then found his way to Canada and eventually married her mother.

Donna's brother Dave was her mentor. He acted in the way she hoped her father would have. He was eleven years older than her. He bought her first bike, a red two wheeled boy's bike. She practiced riding that bike until she had it mastered. Not without many bruises and bleeding as she kissed the pavement numerous times. Later on in life he would buy her first mini-bike. Wow! What an item that was. Dave was crude and harsh in his words, but she always knew he loved her. He ruled with an iron fist and no matter how much a challenge something was, he forced her to continue until she got it right. Even though the boys had a different father than her, it was never as though they felt any less than full-blooded siblings. Dave took her skating and surprised her with a pair of white booted roller skates. They were a big item in that era which allowed her to take lessons and earn herself some pins of accomplishment.

The younger of her two older brothers Dean, left home at fifteen. He was feisty as heck and was always on her father's blacklist. She was ten years younger than Dean and she felt his absence daily. He and her sister left some records at home, which she played daily for years like Elvis Presley and some other big names which inspired her in her teen years. Years later, she and her boyfriend Kenny took a tour bus to see Elvis' second last concert. It was her first big concert and she found it comical when they boarded the tour bus to find every man looking like an Elvis double. There were small, big, thin, heavy and every type of Elvis possible. All the way there the crowd sang nothing but Elvis tunes. Kenny and Donna had no idea that people drank alcohol on bus tours and the whole group was happy to share their loot. The driver stopped when they entered the U.S. so they could purchase their own liquor. She was surprised at Elvis' huge size and how he cried during each song. She had no idea at that time; she was watching a legend as she was snapping one picture after another. He seemed to be a man who had everything except true happiness. That trip would become a fond lifetime memory for her, and she learned that all the riches in the world could not buy happiness.

Donna knew there was a serious problem in her family. She cried herself to sleep almost every night. She was sad and she missed her brother. She was a bed wetter and she tried so hard not to be. It didn't seem to matter what she tried, nothing worked. She felt as though she was weak or had something wrong with her. Her mother was always very patient and she was never scolded. This made her feel terrible since she knew that it was work to do the wash every day. At one point the Doctor gave them some type of medication, which would turn her urine red. It never helped anyway. When she awoke and saw the bright red soaked bed, she was terrified. She wet the bed until she was twelve years old and was mortified that any of her friends would find out the truth. She avoided sleep overs and when she did have them, she rarely slept. One time when she finally had a friend over the terror hit her. She woke up and the bed was soaked. This girl was quite a school bully and the thought of the torment this would cause her was overwhelming. She quickly took the plug out of the hot water bottle which she slept with for warmth. What a relief when her friend woke up and realized the *water* all over the sheets.

Donna was always in fear of her father hurting her mom. The house was always full of screaming and cursing when her dad came

3

home. There had been so many beatings that the boys took from her father. He had beaten Dean so bad that he couldn't walk for two weeks. Her father emitted daily anger against one of the boys. If it were not against them, it was against her mother. She frequently heard him call her mother a "courva, whore", in his own mother tongue, in his fits of rage which he thought she could not understand. Little did he know his baby girl was absorbing all of those choice words. It was Dave who was always there to rescue them when they ran to safety—all thirteen or more times over the years. Times such as Christmases her father would explode, her birthday parties or any random day of the week. Her dad locked her and himself in her parent's bedroom. Screaming once again in his mother tongue that he was going to kill her and himself. She knew he wouldn't hurt her. He loved her. It was simply a ploy to torment her mother. It was then that her mother translated the words to Dave. Dave kicked in the door and took her to safety once again.

When Donna walked into a room and saw her mom and dad in a steamy embrace, she would scream with all of her might. Someone would always come running. She couldn't understand if he was hurting her or not. She couldn't recognize the difference between *affection* and *abuse*.

Chapter 2

On occasion her father would take her mother out; on this particular evening he had taken her out dancing. Donna's brother Dean was left to babysit. Dave was out with his friends. Donna was five years old and Dean was fifteen. In his attempt to entertain her, he decided that they would take a ride on her father's motorcycle. This was a huge risk, as Dean was never allowed to ride it. Things were going well and they were on their way back down the driveway to their home when her foot got lodged in the spokes of the back wheel and stuck against the hot muffler. In excruciating pain and with a foot that looked like it had just come out of a meat grinder, her brother hurried her over to his friend's place, whose mom was a nurse. The woman cleaned her wounds to the best of her ability; wrapping them in gauze and suggested Dean take her to the hospital. At this point fear was ruling him and surely all he was thinking about was the beating that he was going to get when his stepfather got home. Donna was feeling awful for her brother. He always looked out for her and now this had to happen, what rotten luck!!

When her parents arrived, she was laying on the couch in deep pain under a blanket to hide the leg. The pale white color on her face signaled something wrong to her mother. She was beside herself, but the big surprise was her dad. All he did was listen, shake his head, turn around and head off to bed. Mom took her to the hospital. The gauze that the woman had put on her wounds had soaked up a lot of blood and had dried onto the mangled flesh. She would never forget the hard time they had at the hospital getting it off, slowly peeling back the gauze that was being loosened with syringes of water. It turned out she had second degree friction burns from her ankle to her knee. Donna was a year in a full leg cast and with all her luck she caught chicken pox. She had to put up with the itch, using one of her mom's knitting needles to scratch with down inside the cast.

One night while she was bathing upstairs, her father arrived home in a drunken stupor and in a mad fury. She could hear the screams of 'courva' with his deep loud voice all the way up stairs. Her mom ran into the bathroom and quickly wrapped her in a towel. It was evident they were in trouble. Her mom carried her as she ran next door through knee-deep snow to the neighbors for shelter. The snow burned Donna's damp skin when her mother dropped her during the trek. She could not stop the trembling that overtook her body. It stopped when they arrived at her sister's home sometime later for security. She didn't understand why this was happening. Why were they being punished?

They moved to an apartment where she would start a new school. It wouldn't last longer than three months. She had befriended a young girl named Sherri, who was confined to a wheelchair. Donna thought Sherri was so pretty with her black rimmed glasses. She was sorry to move back home, since she enjoyed their walks to school together and she felt proud to push Sherri's wheelchair along the sidewalk to school. She learned to be thankful for what she had, and for being able to run and jump. She was grateful to have met this happy little girl.

On her sixth Christmas she was so excited over her new Timex watch, she ran about the house to find her parents. Her mom was in her bedroom, lying on the bed, totally paralyzed and silent. Donna never really knew what happened, but she remembered vividly that an ambulance took her mom away as Dave told her she would be ok. He would look after her. Donna was later sent to stay with her mom's friend Helen. Her father came the next day and told her that her mom was going to die. She had no idea why he would say that. Shortly after this, two days later she was taken home to her mother.

Donna walked into the kitchen of their two-story home. She let out a screaming cry for help as she saw her Mom's arms wrapped around a man, and a steamy kiss was taking place. Hands came over her mouth quickly to stop the cries. It *wasn't* her father! She was so confused.

Her parents finally divorced when she was eight years old. Even though Donna was a young child she felt the relief of a now quiet home. She felt safe not only for herself but also for her mother.

Years after her father's death, Donna would find the family which remained on his homestead in the Ukraine. She had done a search through the Red Cross and because they had previous information on someone in the Ukraine, trying to find her father, they completed the search. She picked up the large brown envelope from their mailbox and was excited to see the return address from the Red Cross. When she tore open the envelope the picture of her father was a pleasant surprise for her. Somebody knew her father. Donna had found family—the chubbier than normal photo of her father, turned out to be his brother. She could have sworn they were twins. Her uncle had lived his life in England since the war. She now had established contact through mail and would later make a phone call to find out more about this family connection.

Chapter 3

*D*onna's mother had met a nice Christian man, Bill, who had two daughters of his own. They moved into Bill's small home when Donna was in the middle of grade 3. Her bedroom was the porch surrounded by windows where ice formed along the wall in winter. She was cold a lot and her mom gave her a hot water bottle to sleep with every night. She knew when she got older and bought her own house, she would never be cold. Dave was soon to marry and she was also going to have a step-sister. Lila took Donna under her wing, always seeming very protective of her. She was sixteen years old and became a young mother, which took her out of their home and into her own. Donna seemed to recall a fair amount of friction between Lila and her father. Not the closeness that he shared with his other daughter Dar, who was three years older. Dar was Bill's oldest daughter and she married at nineteen. She was already out of the house and creating a life of her own.

Donna had made a friend named Ronnie who was intellectually challenged. Her mother had brought many of these children home for holidays as their families often left them in the institute where she also worked. Ronnie's dad was a prominent lawyer in Winnipeg and they had thanked Donna for being nice to him. Most of her friend's picked on him and she hated the sad feeling she got when she witnessed this as she was taught not to ridicule but to love. She was walking home with Ronnie one day. He had received a "five star" sticker and he wanted to show her. She praised him for his good work then suddenly he hit her over the head with a 7-Up bottle. She felt a bit dizzy but quickly got her wits about her and ran as fast as she could back towards the school. Her mother was called at work and she came home. Donna was heartbroken since she never ever picked on this young boy. She learned that people don't always mean to do what they do. Ronnie didn't know the difference between praise and ridicule.

It was late and very dark outside when the sound of breaking glass instilled a fear in all of them that were inside the house. Donna's father, in a drunken rage had walked through the garden and had thrown a huge rock through the back window. He was never caught, even though his footprints were in the garden. He remained *unpunished*.

She would have scheduled visits with her father, where they would most often go shopping. He bought Donna, her first 45 and some nice treasurers that little girls liked. Her father often drank with relatives of her mom. This time he would take her to her mother's aunt. Donna was to call home but the adults monitored her call as they drank alcohol. Her father told her not to tell her mom where she was. Her aunt stood guard and she was uncomfortable not being able to speak freely. She believed her dad had planned to mentally torment her mom once again. He told her they were going to spend the night there. Donna never had overnight visits with her father and she was clever enough to realize that they were not doing things right. When the adults were in the other room she called a taxi, walked out of the house and took a cab home. Visits were supervised after that. She lost touch with her father after their next move.

They were to move again and Donna was happy to leave the small cold house. She had been picked on a lot by cruel kids because she had a stepfather and because they were Ukrainian. She had a new home now. The house was larger and close to her sister's where they had visited often. She had made a lot of friends in the area and was starting Junior High School. Many of the kids from Headingly came to her house during lunch hours since they were bussed into the city for school.

There was something strange in this house. She had invited two friends to spend the night and they slept up in the attic room. Donna and her friends were becoming quite drowsy, when all of a sudden they sat up, looked at each other and then ran with all their might down the stairs. They all crammed into her single bed petrified. They never knew why other than they all felt a chill while goose bumps ran up their arms. Her mom and Bill had experienced their own chills, but never told her about it until she was older. They had rented the upper level to Rose, a nice Christian lady. She stayed only a few months and moved out rather abruptly. Apparently the cabinet doors upstairs would always be open when anyone arrived home. This was strange because at many times it was like they were nailed shut and no one could open them. They moved after one year and the house was always filled with new owners. A few years later that house was demolished.

They settled into her hometown of Headingly. Donna was thrilled to be moving there. The trees along the winding river road formed a tunnel; it was lush and always smelled fresh. It reminded her of a painting. She spent a lot of time out there with the friends she had met at school. Her best friend Elaine lived three houses away. These would become some of the best years of her life. Of course with the best, also comes the worst. Just one year after they moved there, she found herself in constant companionship of her girlfriend Kathy's brother, Kenny. He and Donna were to become a couple, so when Elaine asked her along on a summer trip to Saskatchewan, she declined. Summer was a lot of fun in Headingly. She spent most of her days at Kenny's parents' farm. Donna loved to help in their huge garden. His mother always baked and had home cooked meals. Who could resist fresh buns and real butter? It was a lifestyle she loved. Even when they stole wine from the attic and she puked her guts out, hanging over the sump pump for three days, she loved the farm.

Kenny's father was a staunch old German with stringent rules. When he went off to town, they would all head down to the river for a swim, always finding the old man to return far too early with his harsh punishment for slacking off on chores. It seemed as though every kid in town spent time out at the farm eager to help with painting the granaries and barns in exchange for Kenny, Kathy and the younger brothers being granted permission to head to the beach. Kenny's dad had told Donna he liked her since she was one of a few people who could look him in the eye. Little did he know she was scared to death of him but was never going to let him know that. She spent years in the company of Kenny's family and they created many fond memories.

It was Kathy who came with her a few years later to visit her father. Donna wanted to visit him and thought of getting to know him better. He was of course, drunk again and asked her why Kathy was so fat. She was crushed since Kathy was quite obese and regardless of her weight they had formed a very strong friendship. Her father spoke in broken English and was becoming intolerable. Forgetting who she was at one point, he grabbed Donna's crotch mumbling something obscene. He was so drunk that he forgot she was his own daughter. She didn't see her father again for quite a few years.

One day, the neighbor girl, who was known for greatly exaggerated stories, hammered on the door.

"I heard Elaine died", Val sobbed.

"Bull shit", Donna hollered as her anger rose up instantly at such a terrible lie!

It was no lie. Elaine had died of heart failure while she was in the outhouse at the age of fifteen. A friend of theirs, Kim had found her, making this, the saddest day of Donna's life. Elaine's death hit Headingly like an atomic bomb. They were all absolutely devastated to lose such a close friend. Elaine's mother had lived most of her years in Headingly, a deaf mute, whose husband had died a long time ago. She ended up moving to Saskatchewan with her oldest daughter. They remained in touch and Donna visited whenever she passed through. Elaine's death was to create such an impact on her life that she found everything a challenge for a long time afterwards. She thought of Elaine daily. She didn't understand why such a good person couldn't live a longer life. She later chose to believe that maybe Elaine was rewarded for being that good person. Donna realized that death was not necessarily *punishment*.

Chapter 4

*D*onna's brothers chose never to indulge in alcohol, ever. Even though they grew up in the era and hung around with boys that were experimenting with both drugs and alcohol.

Her older sister was seventeen years her senior. Dorien drank along with her father and grandmother. She chummed with the boys who would later be known as "The Guess Who", "B.T.O." and various others. But it all took its toll on Dorien a beautiful, blue eyed, platinum blonde who later in life, turned into a pathetic, alcoholic recluse. She lived in an abusive marriage with both alcohol and pills playing a huge part in her life. Many years before Donna's niece had told her of some unhealthy events that were happening in the home. She could hear her mom yelling for help but was forbidden to enter the room. She told Donna of her father coming into her bedroom and tickling her young budding breasts. Donna told her mother, since she could recall him gesturing similar offensive innuendoes towards her at a town dance while she had been visiting their home. He had asked Donna to a slow dance with him. She thought nothing of it until he whisked her to the other side of the room. She could feel his tongue in her ear. Not quite sure how to handle this she twisted her head away from him as she anxiously waited for the dance to end. He laughed a drunken laugh. The husband suddenly vanished from their remote northern community, apparently searching for work but never returning again.

Donna's grandmother sent them by plane to bring Dorien home. Dorien was a living hell!! She was uncontrollable as they tried to pack what little they could take on the plane. There were only two ways in to the north—plane or train. Donna had enough of the battle with Dorien even though she was petite; she found strength to throw Dorien over her shoulder. Dorien was so drunk that she bit Donna's butt as she carried her into the living room. Donna dropped her, butt first into a big cardboard box where she sat for hours with her legs straight up in the air, unable to get out. Cruel as it seemed, Donna couldn't help but crack up laughing as she watched her sisters legs wiggle above the box. She called out for her mom to come see. It was hilarious in her eyes.

Her mother was silent as Donna called from the other room asking what items they should pack. No response, found her checking the bedroom where her mother sat motionless with a blank expression.

Donna asked again, "What's wrong?"

She took the album from her mother's hands. My God she thought in silence. There were pictures of her sister; she appeared unconscious, in different sexual positions with objects where they did not belong. Carrots and other items were clearly visible. Dorien's husband was a sexual deviant along with his brother. His brother's wife had ended up in a psychiatric ward many times and was never the same beautiful woman she once was.

A while later s Donna locked Dorien in the bathroom. Dorien was uncontrollable and was always trying to run away. Donna could hear the noise and decided to see what Dorien was into now. She had gotten stuck in the bathroom window of the trailer with her butt and legs being the only parts visible. They all had to laugh at this one. Donna learned that laughter was the best medicine. Without it they surely would have lost their minds.

Donna started to remember one time when she was babysitting her niece and nephew back in Winnipeg. She was cleaning Dorien's house as she often did when she babysat. She couldn't stand the clutter that was constant in this home. They were like hoarders. She awoke to her mother and Dorien shaking her to consciousness as she lay across the vacuum hose on the floor. Was she drugged as well? Had she drank a spiked drink? Was this how Dorien had always been knocked out when all the while her husband claimed she was drunk? She never would know the answer.

Both the men in Dorien's life left the northern community and ended up in different provinces. She never recovered from the sick abusive life that they lived. Her husband's sisters had admitted the sexual abuse that they suffered from their own father; however their mother would deny this for the rest of her life. Dorien's husband although wanted by the RCMP, remained . . . . *Unpunished.*

Chapter 5

*D*onna's younger years around Bill, the man she referred to as her stepfather were pleasant enough. This changed when she hit the rebellious teen years. She remained close to her mother during these times as her mom had instilled a fear in her. A fear, that if she did anything wrong, her mother would shun her for days on end, a fear that she carried with her until her mother's death many years later.

Donna awoke one morning to a hardness pressing against her leg, far too close to her groin. In her slumbering moments she held Kenny in her thoughts. Then she smelled the foul odor of his breath. It was Bill! She could feel him becoming harder as she pretended to be asleep. Not quite sure what to do since she knew they were home alone. She took a deep breath and turned over making sure to knee him hard where he would be certain to feel it. He quietly rolled out of her bed and crawled out of her room. The incident was not discussed.

Bill was well liked in the community. He attended church most Sundays, was a light drinker, had a deformed right arm and was a real damn phony! Donna hated Bill after that. To play on a young girl's sexuality and pretend it never happened? Personally, she was embarrassed but most of all very disgusted. One day in a pathetic attempt to justify his behavior, he mumbled something to her about expecting a phone call and being deaf in one ear, he needed to be close to the phone. The phone was next to her room and it was easier to hear the phone from her room however that still didn't justify him being in her bed. She often wondered why his youngest daughter moved far away and hardly remained in contact. He had raised his two girls alone with the oldest remaining in fairly close contact. It had always seemed kind of odd, Donna was never quite sure exactly what it was, but she saw things clearer, with Bill and quietly praised his youngest daughter for leaving him. She began to rebel at anything he demanded. When he ordered her to do something, she disobeyed. At one point she ended up with him holding her by the neck with his fist threatening her face.

"Go ahead, my brothers will kill you"! She screamed.

He let go, declining any further confrontations.

Donna's mom worked full time and never witnessed any of the conflict between them. Her mother and Bill had begun their own confrontations. Her mother paid for almost everything. She earned more income allowing her to manage her funds accordingly. Bill got involved with another church, a cult as it turned out to be the Hari Krishna's. He gave a portion of his income until her mom and he came to verbal blows regarding this group. He later joined another new church. This one was a version of the Moonies which was a cult headed by the Reverend Sung Yung Moon. As Donna grew older she studied books about cults and was fascinated at how people could become brainwashed. It would never happen to her!

Bill hauled water that was stored in a holding tank and he would limit Donna's bath water to two inches. It was the one expense he agreed to pay. He had it timed, and knew how long it took to reach an acceptable level. He would then shut the breaker off, which would in turn stop the water pump. With shampoo in her hair Donna would bale the bath water with a cup to rinse out the suds. On winter days she would keep pouring the water over her body to warm herself up. It was a challenge with two inches. She was thankful that she didn't have to heat the water as well. Soon she could master bathing in minutes. She vowed when she left home and had her own place, that her baths would be filled to the top. Bill had a nail in the wall at 67 degrees F on the thermostat. They could never turn it up any higher. Donna also vowed that she would never be cold when she moved out. Memories of being cold always had her dreaming of warmth and tropical climates like Jamaica. She had never been, but one day she would. Perhaps she would move to the tropics someday and never be cold again. The thought was always a dream of hers.

Chapter 6

Kenny and Donna had broken up. They were young and craving to explore the world ahead of them. Donna started to date his older cousin Matt. Matt was handsome as heck she thought. He had dark curly hair with cobalt blue eyes. Being a cousin of Kenny's, he had been raised in a Mennonite family. He was asked to leave his home because his hair was touching his ears and he refused to cut it. This was the era of long hair. Only geeks, nerds and army boys sported short hair. Matt was a nice guy and drove a cool car. They dated a short time, partying and living life.

On their way into a party, Donna said hi to a boy that she had had a crush on. The crush was short lived and she damn near was as well. Matt threw her into the car and drove the car straight into the ditch. He was furious. She should not have acknowledged the guy at the party. She was one that always spoke to everyone but being the social butterfly certainly did not pay off this time.

Matt was very drunk and acting like a wild man. When they arrived at her house, Matt proceeded to pull out his hunting rifle and decided she was fair game. Bill and Donna's mom had a struggle with him to get the gun. Bill pulled out the pin and threw it in the river . . . Donna hid under the couch in the living room. Matt slept off the rye whisky, which obviously had not agreed with his chemistry.

Matt attempted the whisky another time at a social evening in Headingly. All was fun and games until another guy said hello to her and Matt decided that they should go out and get some air. They got air all right, as he lifted Donna up and threw her into a wall. One of the hometown boys saw what was happening and gave Matt a taste of his own medicine. Matt had a sad upbringing and wanted someone for his very own. He felt extreme remorse and told her how his brothers had always pulled guns on their wives in fits of alcohol filled rages. Donna remembered his sister in law confiding in her such a story. Her husband had dragged her outside and held a shotgun to her head because she had been wearing short shorts. Donna would have been killed years ago she told the woman since she wore tiny bikinis; lipstick and she dyed her hair. Without alcohol, Matt was a kind, caring hardworking man. He quit drinking whisky.

Donna's family had decided it was time for her to take a quick vacation, so she took the train to Edmonton to visit her brother Dean. She found herself looking over her shoulder daily. Always watching people and keeping her back to the wall. She was used to the mild manner of Kenny and frankly Matt had scared the hell out of her. She refused to go anywhere except to work with her brother and she regretted her split with Kenny. He was a gentle and kind person. She was very upset and embarrassed when Dean tried to set her up on dates. When people at his work commented about his good-looking wife, he would sarcastically mention that she was his kid sister. He would make it very clear that she was available. As much as she loved her brother, she loathed the cockiness he displayed. She knew that deep down he was proud of her.

Easter was always a special day for their family. Donna's mom rarely had time to home cook meals during the week because she worked full long days. Holidays were always filled with tons of homemade food, plenty of drinks and always a houseful of friends.

This was like Christmas dinner for them at her mom's house. Donna was excited when she called home. She knew she would be missing the great feast.

She was disappointed that there was no answer and was sure they must be at her brother Dave's. Dave answered the phone and was very quiet when she happily said hello. When Donna asked if her mom was there he replied softly saying "Yeah, she's here." The monotone voice instantly signaled to her that something was wrong

"Let me talk to mom" she demanded.

She was relieved to hear her voice when her mom mumbled a weak "Hello." Then the sound of crying.

She was terribly confused when Dave was back on the phone and asked to speak with Dean. What were they hiding she wondered. At that moment she witnessed her brother Dean cry for the first time.

"Oh no, poor mom." He muttered.

Donna began to panic; Dean demanded that she "shut up."

"Mom's house has burned down" he said.

She fell to her knees and felt nauseous as she thought of her pet cat charred to death. All of her childhood keepsakes and her cross collection had gone up in smoke along with everything her mother had toiled so hard for. Donna spent the whole day in the bathroom.

They piled in her brother's half-ton truck and headed towards home, to Headingly. Donna felt as though this was a bad dream. She knew when they drove over the hill leading to their house that it would still be there. At the top of the hill she smiled as she saw the house. It was the first house on the street along the riverbank, surrounded by huge oak trees that formed a tunnel over the road. Bewildered, she wondered why everyone told them there had been a fire. As they drove closer she could see it was only the frame of the house against the white sky, which had created a deceiving illusion. Her home was now a pile of ashes, an empty shell, only a pile of rubble left where their house once stood.

Donna found it fascinating that out of the fire, her white bible and her collection of crosses were all unscathed, all 34 of them, which she has to this day. Along with the daughter's pride ring her mom had ordered for her birthday. She hadn't even seen it yet. She learned to cherish the few simple childhood possessions she now had left.

Donna had never been an overly religious girl but she longed to believe in a higher power in which she could seek peace and contentment. She always felt a calling of sorts. Her mother had never really gone to church. Sundays were her mother's only days that she could sleep in. As she grew older, her mom began to hope that there may be some type of a superior being. She was a firm believer in beings from other planets and a true believer of Nostradamus. She would often quote "Native Spirituality". Donna would find herself later in life researching the same as she became friends with a number of aboriginal people. One in particular, who she met by chance, reminded her of mom's friend Helene who they had sent her to for protection in the past. Pauline would become a lifelong friend and mentor. As a child, Donna's father took her to Catholic services. Although an extreme alcoholic, he was a firm Catholic in his mind. She realized that he could do whatever he wanted and then confess it all away. Later she would attend Sunday school by bus always going alone.

When they moved to Headingly, Donna joined the United Church and went alone most times or with Elaine, until Elaine passed away. She joined the choir and was always across from her girlfriends since her voice was lower and she sang alto. On one of the few occasions that her mom came to church, Donna was excited, giddy and mischievous. As her mom sat in the congregation, Elaine and Donna would giggle their way through the hymns. When she lowered her hymnbook to peek at her mom she could see that her mother was absolutely livid. Nevertheless, they continued to giggle.

The townsfolk of headingly held a huge social event to help them with expenses after the fire. This night Kenny and Donna would reunite when it was time for the first dance. She felt weak and a bit lost when Kenny came to her rescue. The neighborhood women held a shower for household items while her girlfriends threw a surprise shower for personal items for herself. Neighbors rented them their old house so they could keep watch on their property that was a few streets away. Water froze inside the house in the barrel that they used for drinking. The wood stove was always bright red with scorching heat surrounding only the first few inches of air. She slept with a hot water bottle for warmth.

When they arrived home one night, Donna's mom was to forget the moment and became very distressed when she noticed the redness of the stove. Heat and flames would cause her to panic. It took them quite a while to calm her down. A portable toilet was not Donna's favorite item on those cold winter days, but they made the best of it all. She pretended they were camping. She was never to forget how compassionate people could be and vowed at this time to try to help others as she traveled through this journey called life. She learned what *little* they really needed to survive and to be happy.

Donna's mother and Bill had a very strained relationship after that. He mother could not understand why Bill did not come to her rescue during the fire. His excuse had always been that he was trying to move the car away from the house. Donna had found the key to the car melted onto the cement driveway when she first arrived home to see the ruins. As her mom was surrounded by flames unable to touch the brass antique door handle, the rollers in her hair were starting to melt. It was in that moment when she screamed, that a firefighter savagely kicked down the door and pulled her to safety. She would later confide to Donna and a few close friends that she thought Bill had deliberately set the fire.

Bill had become involved in yet another religion and held hope that the faith healers in the Philippines would be able to heal his handicapped arm. His sister had dropped him down the stairs as an infant, and his mother had refused to take him to the doctor.

His broken arm never had the chance to develop properly. Bill had planned to use some of the fire insurance money to travel around the world, to the faith healers. When the day of departure neared, he told Donna's mom that he was going alone.

"You can take a trip with your mother or someone else". He said.

It was difficult to see the pained expression on her face and the hurt in her voice. She was so very disappointed and Donna felt so bad for her. Bill had forged her signature at the bank to remove the funds. He had convinced the banker that her mom was home sick. He returned a month later after his travels . . . still handicapped. Bill and mom eventually parted ways. Shortly after he had a new woman.

Many years later, on a visit home to Headingly with her baby daughter, Donna and her husband were in the back seat of her in-laws car. They could see Bill outside in the yard, which was once her home. Her Mother-in law suggested they stop.

"You really should stop and say hello." she strongly suggested.

People didn't really know that Bill was anything other than a nice gentle man.

Donna looked at her husband for support. She had told him about the incident in her bed and he was totally disgusted, however he remained silent. No one else knew about this and they stopped to say hello. She felt an overwhelming urge to spit in Bill's face. It was obvious that he felt uneasy as he invited them inside. Donna declined. He offered to baby-sit so they could go out. She felt the urge to slap him. She was bitter that he ended up with their house. The house that her mom toiled so hard for. Years later she was relieved to see the house was removed, due to road allowance regulations.

Chapter 7

*I*t was time for Donna to leave the nest. Her sister had moved back from the north with her two nieces and her nephew. Donna moved into an apartment in the city. Her niece was four years younger than her and they were like sisters. The life in which her niece and nephew lived was sad and heartbreaking. Her sister Dorien was a daily drunk and abusive at the best of times. She had become addicted to codeine as well as alcohol. Dorien had agreed to sign legal custody over to her. Donna was now the legal guardian of a 13 and 15 year old at 19 years of age. She worked with her mom in her salon, but she received no other funds to help provide for the kids. Kenny helped her as much as possible. He was an exceptional supportive young man. They were far too young, and she had bitten off far more than she could chew. She always felt it was her responsibility to look after their family and she accepted every challenge that was thrown her way. She thrived on helping anyone.

Dorien would call, in a drunken stupor at all hours. Donna found this overwhelming while trying to maintain the teen's school schedule along with her work. She went over to Dorien's house for her weekly check on her. Dorien lay on the couch next to the large brown circle on the carpet that had become the ashtray for her fallen cigarettes. It always amazed everyone that Dorien never had a fire. There was a strong stench this visit and Dorien's words were mumbled and garbled. Her eyes remained closed as she rambled verbal diarrhea. Donna knelt down and lifted her sister's eyelid with her finger. She was surprised to see her pupil was completely square and no iris was visible. She recognized this as a head injury and took Dorien to the hospital. Dorien was about to have emergency surgery for a blood clot on her brain. Her mom was away and Donna was responsible to sign the legal papers. She felt uneasy and worried about Dorien if something should happen. When her surgery was over, she went in to see her and was sickened to see that in the recovery room while still under anesthetic, Dorien had raised her hand to her mouth as though she was smoking.

The following day Donna went to visit her and was taken aback to find out Dorien had signed herself out of the hospital. She immediately drove to Dorien's house and found no one home. She found Dorien with a kerchief covering her shaved head, walking into the liquor store. It was at this point that Donna gave up on her sister ever recovering. She had laughed, cried, begged and pleaded for her to accept help. Dorien agreed to go into a dry out center but reneged when it was time to go. Donna's father and sister were becoming unbearable with the constant calls and demands. The burden became too much.

Donna spoke to Kenny and the teens about leaving the city and they decided they wanted to stay. Her nephew was very upset that she would leave Kenny. Many years later, at her niece's wedding, he thanked her for helping to raise him. He told her that if it weren't for her, he wouldn't be the man that he had become. She was so proud of him. That was one of her biggest rewards to hear his grateful words.

She learned then that sometimes rewards come long after the task, and that we can be fulfilled from the smallest acts of kindness, which we try to pass on to others. She also learned that we cannot always help someone unless they are willing to help themselves and that we alone cannot heal the world.

Chapter 8

*D*onna had always wanted a motorbike, since she had graduated out of the mini-bike that her brother Dave had bought for her. That was one of the most exciting things she ever owned. Of course with Dave's instruction, followed by many sprained body parts and wounds, she had become quite a confident rider. Her father had made a decision that he was giving her a gift. It was a brand new motorbike. His choices were far too large when they went shopping for this new toy. Donna was a petite woman hardly ever reaching 110 lbs. There were not many bikes at that time that would allow her feet to touch the ground. She opted for a 250 Suzuki. She was pretty darn excited about this and when she went to tell her mother, the excitement quickly disappeared. Her mother's disappointment was very obvious and was not anything that Donna had ever anticipated. She supposed since her father had never given any child support as she was growing up, her mother thought this gift was inappropriate. She kept the new bike and eventually moved up to what she considered a bigger and better bike. Donna could dress like a lady, and at the same time, remain the feisty rebellious woman that was born into her.

She set out in search of a home, something and someplace better. Donna stopped in Saskatchewan to visit some of the hometown boys. It was to become an extended visit. She eventually married one of them. Dallas and her had secret crushes on each other throughout some of their school years. Most of their friends back in Headingly, saw right through them. During their time in Saskatchewan they were drawn closer to each other. Her feelings for him were uncontrollable and the excitement of being on her own was overwhelming. Being close to Dallas created far more than butterflies in her stomach. They were consumed with each other. They spent all of their time together. It was exhilarating to be away from their home town and on their own. It was a fun youthful party time in their lives. They stayed in a small town where they started a new life of sorts. They would later move to a larger city close by so she could continue her career as a stylist. Kenny eventually moved to Alberta. They remained friends for many years and attended each other's weddings.

On their visits home to Winnipeg, her now—husband, Dallas would come with her to see her father. She had tried to rekindle a relationship with him but socializing always involved drinking a bottle of vodka, without mix, chased by cherry whisky. He would boast that the bottle he purchased for their visits was only the best and mixing it would ruin it. It was on these visits she would tell her husband since he was much bigger than she that he would have to be the one to keep up with her father.

It was rather funny at times to have to guide her six-foot plus hubby out to the car because her father had drunk him under the table. He was a good sport and Donna was grateful because she knew she would be very sick if it was her who did the drinking. It was considered an insult not to join in the boozing and she often dumped her drink when her father's head was turned.

Not long after the latest visit, the RCMP drove into their driveway as they were visiting with friends. Donna knew instantly why they were there. As she walked out to greet them, the Constable was young and had a strained expression on his face. He found it difficult to look at her when he spoke.

He asked her if she was Donna Campbell.

Without answering his question, she quietly said, "My dad died didn't he?"

"Yes he said. "I'm sorry".

"What happened?" she asked "Who found him?"

She knew her father had few friends and his partner had moved out years before unable to tolerate his abuse. Although the woman had moved out, she had continued to visit him on a regular basis. Donna felt so sorry for the old woman, who had a nervous tremble and suffered severe hair loss. It wasn't surprising given the pathetic state in which her father lived. He would always tell her to shut up and call her a 'courva whore' in his mother tongue. He was meticulous in his dress and kept an immaculate house. He also cooked and ate very well, at the same time drank very well.

The Constable offered little info. Donna walked into the back northern forest of their acreage and took a few moments to reflect. She hadn't called her father for a month. It would be in that month that he would leave this earth. She mourned for the father . . . *that wasn't.*

Donna had to contact the Winnipeg City Police back home and the story was always rather vague. Her father-in-law was a police officer in the city and she felt as though he was trying to protect her from the truth. She found it strange that she would have to go to his detachment to retrieve her father's ID and wallet since it was not in her father's area of the city. No one ever gave her a straight answer as to the cause of death. Even though she had requested an autopsy report on three different occasions, she never did receive one. When she questioned her husband as to what his father might know, he was very vague and claimed that he knew nothing. Perhaps it was in her own best interest not to know the truth. She learned that *what we do not know . . . cannot hurt us.*

Her father's house was always loud and noisy due to his drunkenness. He lived in the suite of a house in the middle of the city that was frequented by prostitutes and vagrants. This week would find silence and undoubtedly a foul odor. He had been dead for five days.

The police had told her that he was found in his bedroom. When Donna arrived at his house, his bed was made and she knelt down to smell the floor beside the bed. There was no odor anywhere and the house was immaculately clean. This would be the first time that there were no liquor bottles in his home. She checked under the carpet where he had always kept hundreds of dollars. There was nothing. Had someone assaulted him while he was in a drunken stupor? Had a prostitute stolen his money? Did he die of natural causes perhaps by withdrawal of alcohol? Many questions remained unanswered. She found a cooked roast beef wrapped in the fridge. Nothing made sense to her.

The funeral director told her that he wasn't sure if he could have an open casket due to the condition of the body. It was May and considerably warm weather at this time of year. They said they would do their best. Donna was content to see her father looked at peace in his casket. She had never planned a funeral before and was at a total loss when she had decisions to make. The funeral director was extremely compassionate. He suggested she purchase an inexpensive casket and use their flower arrangements. She wasn't happy with the casket and chose the next higher in price. Donna buried her father with him holding a single pale white/yellow rose.

Few people showed up at the funeral. Most were Donna's friends, there for moral support. A couple of old drinking buddies arrived and she had no clue who they were. There were not enough pallbearers, so her husband and her brother Dave volunteered, along with one old friend and a man from the funeral home. They struggled with the casket. Her brother Dean didn't bother to come and she understood why. Not only was it not his biological father and to forgive all the beatings would become a lifetime task. She felt so heartbroken, not because of his death but rather because she never really knew him. Donna wondered how one could live this long and have so few people attend the final farewell. Her father's partner approached her at the gravesite. She was furious that Donna had not purchased any flowers.

"How could you do that?" "One little flower!" "Shame on you that is terrible", she spewed.

It was painful but Donna realized everyone has different views. She had thought the single rose was a beautiful gesture. She holds that heartfelt thought to this day and would hope to have the same when she is plucked off this planet. To this day, many of her paintings contain a single pale rose in them.

Donna thought she should write a letter to her father's family in the Ukraine telling them of his death. She tried to explain that even though he ran away during the war, he loved them very much. She told them he suffered for the rest of his life because of the choices he made. His youngest daughter wrote her back and asked Donna how she could say such kind things about a man that deserted his family. She had never forgiven him. They were poor people and although Donna was not wealthy by any means, she sent them used clothing. They had written how two families lived in her father's homestead in the original house without power or water. They had no boots for her father's son to walk to work and two women were the only workers. Donna sent boots and a few dollars for the children. They continued to write and ask for more. When the Russian Regime underwent change, they lost touch and none of her letters were answered. She hoped one day she might be able to travel and see the homeland of her father.

Chapter 9

Johnny appeared at her door many years later when trauma struck in the early years of her marriage. His wife had passed away during the years and they had lost touch. His friendship with Donna's mom continued and they grew closer over time.

Donna's husband had been racing up north when he hit an ice heave and his snowmobile was thrown many feet in the air only to land on top of him as she stood there videotaping the race. At first she didn't believe it was him, but the sled was in first place and he wasn't often second. He stood up and then lay across the seat. The sled was still running and he inched his way across the finish line as the sled that had been trailing behind, passed him just before he crossed the line. Donna had just finished nursing the baby and handed her two-year-old daughter to her girlfriend as she ran in knee-deep snow towards him. She was out of breath and her legs were aching by the time she reached him. He drove back towards the pit with her running behind as she wondered how she was going to make it all the way back. He asked for a cigarette and he hardly complained but admitted awkwardly that he was hurt. Donna knew when he said he was hurt that it was far more serious.

They waited anxiously for the RCMP to arrive. There was no ambulance in this small northern community and he had to sit up in the back of the truck as they drove over a rough pot holed road uphill to the nursing station. The nurse who was a nun was very sympathetic. She knew they had to get him to a hospital quickly. Donna asked the nurse if there was blood in the urine that she tested. The nurse looked at her awkwardly.

"Yes" she whispered.

They waited for the plane that had been called in. With her husband stretched out on the gurney, they could not squeeze him in through the doorway of the plane. A few more minutes and the men would remove the door to get him through. As they stood on the icy lake where the plane had landed, one man slipped while balancing his end of the gurney. He caught his footing, almost releasing his hold on the gurney.

Geezuz, she thought, what next?

As they were flying to the hospital, Donna held her baby in her arms at the same time supporting the gurney with her foot so her husband didn't roll into the cockpit. The pilot casually mentioned that the door latch didn't quite lock too well, so she held a tight grip on the latch the whole flight. She stared out the window in prayer as she took in the beauty and the abundance of the lakes far below them. She described the view and talked as though they were on a trip. What a trip this was to be. Her husband looked nervous, not because of his injuries, but from the fear of flying as he lay there with a paper bag beside him. Donna felt as though she had been given an extra strength—the same strength that she would be blessed with, many more times over the following years.

They arrived in FlinFlon. After flipping her husband upside down on a medical board and doing other tests, the doctor took Donna aside. He told her he felt it was necessary to contact the family. Her husband asked her not to, however she decided to call while they waited for the air ambulance to arrive. He had also been bleeding from the kidneys and the liver. Along with their two-month-old baby, they had been air lifted to the northern Manitoba hospital and then air ambulanced to a major city in Saskatchewan where he would require major back surgery to fuse the broken vertebrae. Their two-year-old daughter was to remain with her girlfriend since the space in the plane was limited. The future looked very bleak.

His parents arrived within 24 hours. Donna's heart went out to them, as they always appeared to be such strong people and showed little emotion, she knew they felt helpless as they waited for more news on their only son. He had five days to make a decision whether he would opt for surgery risking the spinal cord being damaged, or lay in a bed for six months to a year, allowing the bones to self-heal. That would be followed by therapy for muscle loss and he would have to learn how to walk again. When he asked for her opinion, Donna was at a loss. She knew he could barely cope with the five days of bed rest, let alone six months, but she did not want to make the decision. He opted for surgery.

As they waited in the family room Donna often found herself looking into the operating room, only to be removed by a nurse. She was calm but her milk had ceased temporally so she fed the baby glucose water. The five-hour wait seemed like an eternity. It was while she was waiting that another young woman along with her family was brought into the waiting room. The woman's husband had been in an accident and was in critical condition. His whole body was mangled and he needed surgery everywhere. All his major bones were broken and it was not likely that he would survive. Donna found herself not only praying for her husband, but for this woman and her family.

Finally the hardnosed doctor approached her with the bloody gloves, which were dripping onto his white clogs.

"Well, he's a strong man and he's lucky to have such big bones". I'm sure he'll walk again sooner than you expect". "Let her into the room to see her husband", he ordered the nurses.

Donna went into the room where her husband lay resembling a corpse. His skin had never been so pale and the lifted areas where the monitoring tabs had been attached looked as though it were not his own skin.

"I'm here" she said. "How are you feeling?" she asked.

"I feel like a porcupine on the side of the road." He mumbled.

She silently thought, that's pretty much how he looked too.

That night she stayed at a hotel close by with her in-laws. As they left the hospital, Donna broke down for the first time. Her mother in-law put her arm around her and knew she was crying tears of happiness. He would be ok, and he would be home soon. They sat in the hot tub and toasted with a glass of wine. Donna was so grateful that they were there and that they could comfort each other.

She slept most days and nights at the hospital. Her husband would go through terrifying nightmares caused by the morphine. He would hallucinate, pulling out tubes and intravenous. He was angry and difficult. He snapped out of his moodiness when Donna retaliated that she was damn tired of wiping his ass, since that was the nurse's job.

She would often walk to the cafeteria to sit and take a few moments from the hospital ward. It was here a young nine-year old girl approached her.

"Are you sad?" she asked.

"Yes" Donna answered.

Donna told her why and the young girl began to take it upon her sweet self to comfort her. The girl had cancer and was likely going to die. It was then that Donna learned to appreciate each day for what it was, to count her blessings and be grateful for the gift of life no matter how short or long it may be. To be thankful for all the wonderful things she had in her life. She never saw the little girl again.

The babies along with Donna's mom had stayed in a lodge across from the hospital. It was comfortable but it certainly was not home. It was a pleasure to be invited to join in by the Hutterites who were sharing the kitchen. They were a caring bunch and often entertained the two year old. The men would often walk Donna to and from the hospital at night. They found themselves building a friendship in times of need and they remained in touch for many years after. There was nothing else like an authentic Hutterite dinner and she was grateful to have the opportunity to make friends with these people.

Their two year old was very quiet when Donna took her in to see her daddy. He had lost weight and looked pretty rough. She was shy and stand-offish as her daddy looked a bit different. He lay silent when Donna brought the baby in and she noticed a tear in his eye.

In the next few days there was to be a surprise 30th birthday party for Donna held by her baby's godparents. The plans were changed and instead she shared a McDonald's bagged lunch with her husband in his hospital room. Her in-laws had made numerous visits along with her mom. After a grueling month in the hospital, they were back at home and she was very relieved. They had adjusted areas in their small home to accommodate her husband.

Donna's mom was a lot older than most parents of people in her age group. She took on the daring task of bearing a child at 40 years of age. She would always claim it kept her young. Donna's in-laws had recently purchased a store in their hometown and had to make frequent and shorter visits in order to manage their business. It was Johnny who showed up to help with the daily survival. They lived in a small house on an acreage. The old oil furnace had given out, so Johnny helped to chop and stockpile wood. They hauled water from the town well to fill their holding tank, which was their water supply.

Donna went back to work at the Salon where the staff did a wonderful job keeping the business going. However their other venture, a food outlet in their major mall was going down—hill fast. She had given the business to her close friend, a single mother of four to manage. The woman had a hard life with no support for her children. Donna knew between the two of them, that they could watch her grow and eventually become financially secure. They talked how they would prove that she could do it. In the end Donna and her husband lost the store and Donna was devastated. All the money she had saved was invested in the business. It took many years to pay for that loss. The friendship suffered, and she felt that was the biggest loss. She felt sick and sad inside for a long time after. Her friend opened her own restaurant. She closed after one year. Donna learned that trying to help someone, doesn't always go as planned. It's called "Life" she reminds herself.

A year later her husband was back in the affair with the love of his life, his snowmobile. This time they had been out on a ride with friends. Another woman and Donna decided to meet up with them ahead in a vehicle. Donna had an uneasy feeling while they were waiting, since they were taking too long. The other woman sat silent when Donna whispered that she knew her husband was hurt. Her friend assured her that nobody was hurt; rather they were just being boys, which they were. There was a dim light in the distance slowly approaching. It couldn't be her husband, it was far too slow. When the friend's husband arrived, he had difficulty looking at Donna.

"I know something is wrong" Donna said.

"He's bleeding a bit but he's standing and is ok." He replied.

They drove to the scene and once again Donna found herself asking her higher power for strength. She wanted him so badly to be all right, so that she could give him supreme hell! And that she did, as he sat silent. This feisty little woman was really pissed off. He was reluctant to go to the hospital, nevertheless they ended up going. She thought it was for the gash on his forehead but ended up back again the following day due to the pain that he was trying not to acknowledge. He had broken his ankle.

Donna and her husband had driven up a driveway as they were driving around the countryside. There was this beautiful log home with a long driveway in the forest. It was fairly secluded and seemed to be a little bit of paradise.

"I would love to have a home like that one day but I know we never will" Donna said.

"Yes we will" her husband replied nonchalantly.

She was heartbroken when friends visiting their house laughed at how they were being blown across the room from the draft blowing in through the doorframe. Most of their friends had nice homes and she was envious. Her little girl was five when she asked how come they had such a small house. Donna explained that someday they would have a big house like many of their friends.

She had found a home for sale, and the owner was willing to negotiate. It was the beautiful log home! Donna was thrilled. It had closets and everything she thought a home should have. She told her hubby she was moving . . . with or without him. She was cocky as heck.

Donna had never wanted to stay at home, she was a worker and she wanted something to show for it all.

Christmas was here once again and this was the year that was a pleasant surprise. As they exchanged gifts, her husband handed her a wrapped box. He anxiously watched while she carefully opened the handpicked present. Oh, what a surprise she thought with a more than strained expression on her face, as his parents watched. It was the key to the junkiest snowmobile he owned.

"Yahoo", she said sarcastically.

He then commented on the fact that she must be blind. It was then that a glimmer of light caught her eye as she noticed the sparkle attached to the key. He had bought Donna the matching band to her wedding ring. She was overjoyed and burst into tears while she ran into the other room. It was the nicest thing he had ever done. Her father-in-law was wondering why she was crying and asked if she didn't want the snowmobile. She felt for once, that he might really love her. She cherished the ring and later kept it safe for her daughters.

Donna knew how badly her husband wanted a new snowmobile. It was the best thing a man could hope for. Her client, Ann was the one she shared the big secret with. Donna was going to save all year and put a $1000.00 bill in the bottom of her husband's stocking. Ann reminded her how she had to order the bill since no banks in their city stocked them.Donna was frantic that it wouldn't arrive on time. However it did and she was so very excited to place it in the toe of her husband's hanging stocking. He thanked her as he now had his down payment for his new toy. She reached her goal and later in years wished she still had that damn $1000.00 bill.

There was a meeting set for 8:00 and Donna's husband told her to expect him home around 10:00pm. The fluffy snowflakes continued to fall all evening and by late evening, they were having a full-blown storm. Her husband hadn't called and at 1:00am, she began to worry. She watched the clock hit every hour until finally at 5:00am she decided to call his friend who would echo her exact fears.

"Oh no, it's really blowing out there, he's driving your white car and could be rolled in a ditch somewhere and no one would even see him", he rambled.

That was not the response she was hoping for. Once again she wanted him to come home so she could give him heck. She called the police anonymously to ask if there had been any accidents. She was relieved to hear them say there were none. It was 5:00am and Donna was standing outside as if there was something she could do out there. She saw a police car go by and the memory of her father's death flooded back. They must be coming for her she thought, the car drove right by.

6:30am she watched her white car slowly drive in the yard.

"Hi there", he said casually.

Donna was furious. Particularly to see the smirk on his inebriated face.

She started to cry and yelled at him for not calling home. She grabbed the broom close by and whacked him in the arm. Donna went to bed and cried herself to sleep. The following day at work, a delivery boy came in with a bouquet of a dozen red roses. The girls all walked to the door expecting the flowers to be for one of them, since she never got any. They were surprised to see the card addressed to: "Broom Hilda".

"Oh, those will be for me." Donna chuckled.

A hell of a way to finally get flowers she thought, as she held a smile on her face and a chuckle in her heart.

Over the next few years, Donna tired of their lifestyle. She became more and more unhappy. She envied most other women, as she observed the love and attention their husbands displayed. She hoped that someday they could have that together. She was always a very affectionate woman but her husband felt there was a time and place for that. When Donna watched other women receiving gifts of affection, she felt very empty inside. Although she was married, Donna was the loneliest person she knew. She accepted the fact that her hopes of "maybe someday" . . . were really . . . "maybe not".

They were on different paths in this journey of life and they desired different things. Her husband told her that she was an overachiever. He may have very well been correct. Donna felt as though she had been a failure and that whatever she did was never really the right thing. She had become very close to his grandmother. Grandma was such an inspiration in Donna's life. Donna wanted to have a marriage like grandma's and grandpa's. She didn't want to lose grandma and felt as though if they divorced, it would be inevitable. Little did grandma know, it was the strength Donna drew from her that kept Donna in her marriage. Donna's husband couldn't understand why she wanted any change in their lives. Donna laughed as she wondered why anyone did not want this lifestyle to change.

She accepted what she could not change and faced the reality of what she would never have. They eventually parted ways. Neither one of them was to blame, Donna simply felt as though she was never truly loved, and was ready to give up the relationship. It certainly wasn't his fault that she craved what he could and would not give her. Donna wished for him, love, health and happiness. To this day her ex-husband still has his ongoing affair with the love of his life . . . . his snowmobiles.

Chapter 10

*M*onday mornings were generally the Salon's quietest times. Donna was usually there alone, taking the opportunity to catch up on the previous week's paperwork, before the weekend hangovers wore off, and her clients came by to give her all the sordid details. Unlike most people, she loved Monday mornings. Bev worked at the store next door, it seemed like forever and it was always amusing to guess what her mood would be. Bev would either greet Donna before she managed to get to the doorway or remain totally out of sight. Bev was always blunt and to the point. Donna appreciated her openness. Tara worked next door and they became Monday morning coffee buddies where Tara would often lend an ear as if she were a well-trained councilor. At points in Donna's life her support was irreplaceable.

The bells above the doorway jingled. Through a tinted window in the office, Donna watched a dark-haired man carefully close the door behind him and approach the front desk. She couldn't recall seeing him before, yet he looked strangely familiar to her. She studied him for a few moments before going out into the Salon.

"Hi, how can I help?" she asked, looking into a pair of large, piercing green eyes.

"I'm hoping to get a haircut," he said with a strained grin.

For some unknown reason he made her feel instantly uncomfortable. Donna made an excuse that she was too busy to do it right now and asked if he'd mind coming back after 1:00pm, when the other staff would be on duty. He was quite handsome, solidly built and well spoken. She couldn't understand what it was about him that gave her goose bumps, yet she was insistent that he come back later. Reluctantly he agreed to return at 1:00pm.

He offered her a cheerful smile as he walked out the door and said "Have a nice day".

But Donna felt that his piercing eyes were saying something entirely different. To her surprise, he returned at noon. She was sitting at the front desk when he arrived, so she could no longer claim to be too busy to help him. She asked his name. He said it was Alan. Alan Harris. A cold chill ran up and down her arms. She had heard that name many times before. With a penitentiary close by, a woman had to be very cautious about who she conversed with. The small city housed rapists, murderers and pedophiles, many of whom were doing time out on the street due to the overcrowded prison system. As Donna started to cut his hair, she noticed he had a rather solemn look on his face. As often happens in a salon the conversation soon turned to life experiences. Discussion of divorce came up.

Donna had seen the scenario many times before, the painful experience of divorce. She told him that she had been there, done that and that it would get a lot better with time. The conversation was short and he seemed a very intelligent man. He asked about tanning and purchased a package before he left.

The following Thursday Donna was busy in the office and on the floor with clients. As she was chatting with Tom, a longtime client in the waiting area, she turned to see Alan coming towards her from the tanning room. It appeared that Tom and Alan were acquainted. Alan joined in the conversation as though he'd known both of them forever.

When he left Tom said, "That is one sick puppy."

Tom and Donna had met twenty years earlier. His sister had become friends with a school chum of hers from her hometown. Their friendship remained a strong one over the years. Tom worked in the same profession as Alan, played hockey and worked out at the same gym but held absolutely no respect for him and made that very clear to her. He had witnessed far too many outbursts of anger. Alan also had quite a reputation for his aggressiveness on the ice. He rarely made it through a tournament without being thrown out of the game.

Donna ignored the comments, as they all heard trash about people in the salon. She believed everyone is entitled to form opinions and they have to make judgments for themselves. Some of the people that she heard the worst rumors about were the same ones she had come to adore. It had been her experience in the past that most people thrived on idle chitchat and scandalous gossip. At one point when a client asked her about a rumor pertaining to her, Donna added to it, enhancing the story and finding great humour in the end. He had heard she remarried to a local businessman who was a friend of hers. Donna confirmed that she had, even though she wasn't even divorced. The following week the man, her friend, called her and asked what she had been up to now? His phone, along with Donna's had been ringing with curious questions from many people. Many asked why it was kept a secret. They still laugh about that. If it was self-inflicted and about her, Donna thought it was hilarious! When she had been told stories about Alan she felt rather disturbed. There were stories about many other women, from ex-wives to waitresses. She was told about how he stalked women from their city right to British Columbia. It was as though she was being told about a different person. An abusive, controlling man that was very troubled. This person was very angry. Donna thought that she would never allow such deviant behavior into her life, ever! One of her clients who also worked with Alan had told her how back in the 80's there had been a hostage taking and Alan was the hostage. He had been held for 8 hours and most of it at knifepoint. He had said Alan was never the same. There were rumors about sexual abuse during the hours that he was held captive. Who could ever really know?

A few of the staff along with Donna decided that they should walk for an hour or so whenever they could get away. Lina and Donna went for their daily walks. Tara from next door had decided to join them as well. It was therapeutic as well as good exercise. They talked girl talk and shared their thoughts on life. Donna appreciated these gals as her confidantes. On Friday Lina was booked solid, Tara was off, so Donna walked alone. Not long into her walk she saw Alan rollerblading towards her. He had heard them planning their walking time in the Salon. They exchanged hellos and he stopped to remove his blades after which, they walked and talked together, discussing life and situations. He handed her a peach out of his backpack, keeping an apple for himself. How thoughtful she thought. She found it rather hard to believe that this was the same man she had heard so much negative talk about. After all, Alan was a professional with a good career, good looks and from what she could tell from their conversations, intelligent with good morals. Donna always found intelligence in a person to be attractive. Therefore she found people from many walks of life, regardless of their physical appearance, attractive and appealing from within. She had long since learned that a pretty face doesn't mean a pretty heart. She always felt as though she saw through different eyes than most people.

Alan began to show up regularly when Donna went walking, and she began to look forward to her walks hoping that he might appear. She was a single woman and enjoyed listening to the man's perspective on life, his intelligence appealed to her.

During one of the walks Alan told Donna he was heading to his family Island, a thousand miles away for a couple of weeks. He had mentioned how he'd wished he'd known her longer, so that her girls and her could join him. He had already noticed what a sun worshipper she was. She had thought this was rather presumptuous on his part even though the thought of being marooned on a private fifteen-acre island where the sun scorched the rocks beneath one's feet was rather appealing. Donna dreamed of islands but many in the tropics.

The next time Alan stopped at the salon, she was taken aback to see his thick dark locks shaved to near baldness. He reminded her of an inmate and she thought it made his already big eyes, appear bulging and obtrusive. It was obvious that she was surprised by his appearance. Alan said it was a lot easier in the hot sun without grooming his hair and that it would grow back quickly. He said he would call her when he returned.

Chapter 11

*T*hey were at Lina's on Saturday night. The salon staff was having a great time relaxing, indulging and singing along with Karaoke. They knew that they had to be behind closed doors to do that. Artists in their industry they definitely were, but singers they definitely were not. Donna's cell phone rang and she was surprised to find it was Alan. He had just arrived home from the island and she was the first person he called. They caught up on events that happened while he was away. One of his friends had died resulting from a motorbike accident. They talked about it briefly and Donna asked him if he wanted to come join them at Lina's. He accepted excitedly and was there within 5 minutes. Alan's hair had grown back somewhat and he was sporting a stylish short haircut along with a new goatee and a dark mocha tan—he was easy to look at. They had a fun evening with everyone singing and dancing.

Alan extended a lunch invitation to her for the next weekday, which she gratefully accepted. They rarely had time for lunch while at the Salon, but she managed to somehow make time for this. He gave her his address and she was surprised to find that he lived only a few blocks from the Salon.

Lina had mentioned to Donna how she thought there was something in Alan's eyes that she didn't trust. Lina was generally very nonjudgmental and rarely spoke a negative word. She had always been very intuitive in that area, however Donna chose to laugh it off. After all, he and Donna were only walking buddies where she picked his brain and found him to be quite brilliant. Bev had described Alan as trouble along with many other descriptive names. She had known him for years and wasn't pleased to see him in Donna's presence. It bothered Donna knowing that Bev and others felt this way. She did realize that they were simply trying to protect her. She knew that she was fortunate to have such caring friends.

Donna was invited to play pool with Alan and his friend. She was having a rather lucky streak, and the men were seemingly impressed. She found humor in the game and was enjoying herself, which she usually did when she went out. Later they went for a drink at the local spot in town.

Alan had mentioned to her previously that he didn't drink and asked whether that was a problem for her. Donna laughed thinking why on earth would that ever be a problem? At that stage he wasn't her partner and even if he was, a partner who didn't drink sounded quite appealing.

The salon was open late on Thursdays and people often stopped by to visit. The staff usually took this time to unwind and they would all engage in enjoyable fun conversations. Alan stopped in and the girls left one by one until Donna found that they were alone in the salon. She spoke about a man that was a friend in the U.S.A. Alan abruptly cut her off in the middle of her conversation. He made it very clear that he did not want to hear about her friend. He said it bothered him.

"Oh really?" Donna said sarcastically. She was not one to be messed with. She would become defiant and defensive at times like this proving that no one would control her.

Something tweaked inside her at that moment as she thought since she was not in a relationship with Alan, she should be able to speak freely about her male or female friends. Unbeknownst to Alan, this friendship was simply that, and Donna felt it really was none of his business regardless. She felt it rather bold of him to make this demanding statement, however she simply let it pass. They called it a night.

Donna ran into a co-worker of Alan's one day and she took it upon herself to question him personally. She preferred her privacy in their small city. Being cautious and curious at the same time, she had hinted that she might be interested in someone he knew. She wanted to know about Alan.

This man instantly said, "Don't tell me it's Alan Harris"?

He could tell right away that he had guessed correctly. Her face fell awkwardly. His reply caused her to feel uneasy, so she asked for honesty and confidentiality.

"I've never had any problems with Alan but he does have a reputation for being quite aggressive and disruptive. A lot of our co-workers don't have much respect for him." he said.

There were numerous stories circulating around at his work about the abuse and violence he displayed towards his wife before and after their marriage.

"Why would you be attracted to Alan Harris?" he asked.

Then he proceeded to answer his own question.

"Alan is well dressed, like you, has nice hair and works out regularly." he said.

She thanked him for his honesty and candor, but for some reason she could not just end this friendship which had started, to become something more.

Her friendship with Alan continued. After a night of drinks, she made one of the biggest mistakes of her life. They agreed to date exclusively. Now Alan thought she was his! His own personal property. Suddenly, he was everywhere. At her salon daily; her home; her walks; everywhere she went, he was there. One day Donna came home from a long day at work and found him in her flower garden weeding it to pieces. Normally she would appreciate someone weeding for her. She was surprised to drive down her long country lane to see him there. He hadn't called first but chose to surprise her. This was to be the first of many more surprises to follow.

"What are you doing here?" she asked uncomfortably.

"I know how hard you work and I thought I would help you do some chores" he answered.

Donna's parents were coming to town to visit. Alan called her at work and asked if she could stop by his house on her way home. He knew she had a busy schedule and had taken it upon himself to cook lasagna and rolls for her parents and her. What a nice thoughtful thing to do, she thought. The trap was being set but it was too late . . . she was about to be caught.

Her mother was in awe!

"What a sweet man, wow . . . good looking too". She said.

Even though her mother admitted later that his name, cut at her insides, when Donna called home and told her what it was. For it was the same name as her father, Alan. A very abusive alcoholic who left their souls scarred for life, from the trauma that he inflicted upon their family. But her father had been dead for many years and her new papa, a long time life friend of her mom's was a saint in her eyes. They believed history did not repeat itself. Why would any woman deliberately choose a man like her abusive father with the same name? Even if her grandfather's name was also Alan. No . . . . they didn't believe the history theory, even if there were three Alan's.

Tom, her longtime friend often stopped in at the salon to chat. This day he came in and took her aside. He had seen Alan and Donna at the movie rental store.

"What the hell were you doing with Alan Harris?" he asked disturbingly.

"We were going to watch a movie." She said.

"He's a fucking psycho! Stay away from him, he's bad news. He's a sick man!" he scowled.

Her jealous protective friend, she thought. He also told her of other disturbing facts which she said she did not want to hear. As always happens in life, hindsight is 20/20. She should have listened.

The relationship blossomed and all the kindness that Alan showed towards Donna's family and herself kept her thinking that maybe she had found a man like her papa. He was kind, affectionate and very attentive. The romantic sexual moments were beyond anything she had imagined and the sexual attraction between them was a force to be reckoned with. When she saw Alan her body ached in a way that was new to her. She couldn't seem to control her own urges. She wanted him so bad.

These were the qualities she had craved all her life. She had found love. Wow, she was truly blessed!

Chapter 12

While visiting at Alan's home one day, he told Donna that he had something for her. He came out with a crinkly wrapped gift. He apologized for the wrapping, suggesting that it was all he had.

"This is something that I bought a while back on a trip, not knowing who would ever get it. I think it's really beautiful and it will really suit you." he said.

As Donna opened the tattered wrap, she found a beautiful white, Battenberg linen lace dress. It was definitely her taste and she was pleasantly surprised. She thought it was strange that anyone would purchase a dress on one's travels for a person that didn't exist in one's life yet? How could she question such a thought? She humbly thanked him. (. . . much later she believed that this dress was returned to him from another woman that he previously stalked.)

It was only a few months into the courtship and they were talking about many things. In the middle of the conversation Alan begged her to let him give notice on his rented apartment. They had been talking about a completely different topic when he said, "After all, we're together all the time."

She replied "Ya Ya," and continued on with the original topic.

He took that as her consent, and he called in his notice, wasting no time. He would hire a truck and move in the very next day.

Alan was moving in, when Donna arrived home from work. She felt a sick, knot in her stomach. It felt as though she was making a terrible mistake. At the time she chose to believe that he had treated her well up to that point, even though he had demanded she cut contact with her male friends. She could never go anywhere without him. He called her salon, her cell and home numerous times a day. If she had planned a visit with friends, he would simply appear. He would schedule time off his work or be sick to ensure that he was always by her side. Donna believed he loved her more than anyone ever had. After all, he just wanted to be by her side all the time and he would be disappointed if he couldn't reach her. He needed to do EVERYTHING with her; she couldn't be alone, even with her own children. That meant trips and holidays she had planned before he was in the picture now needed to be altered.

Donna and her children had saved hard for two years for their trip to Disneyland. She wanted to give her girls a happy life. She wanted so badly to create memories of the things she only dreamed of as a child. Donna worked hard and knew she could give them a good life. They were her whole life, her reason for being. Alan joined them on the trip and for the most part, they all had a great time.

The highlight seemed to be their day trip to Mexico where the girls witnessed the poverty and the happiness of the Mexican people. Donna admonished them about giving away all their pesos to the beggars, however the compassion in their young hearts could not be harnessed and they came home peso free. They learned a huge life lesson in giving and sharing. To this day they always take their used clothing and some extra school supplies on every trip, the girls make sure of that. They had learned to be compassionate at a young age.

On their way back to L.A. they hit a traffic jam and Donna saw an angry, extremely loud and nasty side of Alan.

"Stupid fucking idiots!" he screamed. "Get the fuck out of the way you whores!"

She was in shock! As the girls sat quietly in the back, Donna asked that he let them out. It was very hard to sit and listen to the vulgarity. He had the loudest voice she had ever heard in her life. It was frightening. Surprisingly, it was much the same as her father's would be when he would come home in his drunken stupors—the ones where he would call her mom a whore and quite often cause them to flee from their home. Donna had not heard that word since she was a child. Alan was rambling on and on, all about a traffic jam. He appeared to be out of his mind. There was tension on the way home and she realized that this seemingly caring man could be a tad scary when angry.

Chapter 13

Donna got the phone call while they were out shopping. Her mom had suffered a stroke. The girls, Alan and Donna immediately drove to her hometown. They arrived nine hours later. Her mom was doing well, and as Donna slept beside her she feared that she might actually lose her mother. When her mother opened her eyes and looked over she was shocked to see Donna and cried. Donna loved her mother.

Alan knew Donna was feeling down after her mother's stroke. Many times she had contemplated moving back to the city where she grew up. She was a mother now with a business and many responsibilities so it wasn't that easy. She felt as though she was trapped here in this city, away from her family until her children were grown. Donna had been shuffled from school to school as a youngster and she wanted stability for her children. It was enough that she was divorced. It was their home and she longed for them to feel secure. She vowed to give them a good life.

Alan chose to tell Donna of the birthday gift he bought for her.

"We're going to Mexico and you have five days to prepare" he said anxiously.

"Wow . . . are you kidding?" she asked excitedly.

She had gone every year since her divorce. Donna thought it was her reward, since she didn't smoke or lead an extravagant life. She always searched for seat sales and was successful every year as was Alan this year. $180.00 return—Although she felt guilty since she knew Alan paid huge child maintenance fees to his ex-wife. He also had previous debts and worked many long hours to make ends meet. She thought it strange, though she never questioned why a man with an above—average income had so little to show for it.

Donna learned later about the torment he inflicted on his ex-wife and the history regarding his marriage. Not to mention the quick annulment, which he received in his first marriage. There had been two ex-wives, both of which had suffered from his anger and abuse. She would learn later that Alan had a lengthy file at the police station from previous incidents over the years.

They walked in the scorching sun along the sandy beach. Alan was extremely happy. He appeared to be high on life.

He turned to her on the shore and said, "Donna, will you marry me?"

She laughed and remained speechless. This came from out of nowhere.

"Not right away, but will you marry me?" he repeated.

"I'll be engaged and live with you, but that's as committed as I get." she said.

Donna had long ago lost faith in marriage and since she had never planned to have more children, she felt no need to have a legal bond.

They were lying on the beach in Mexico, basking in the blazing sun when Alan brought her a pail of beer.

"Wow, a whole pail? How much do you think I'm going to drink?" she giggled.

He laughed and said "It's cheap and the bottles are small."

A while later he bought another pail of three. She turned towards him and asked what he was doing as she watched him guzzle a beer.

"I feel like having a beer," he defiantly murmured.

Okay, she thought, this could be interesting. And it certainly was. Alan decided to follow up with tequila. Oh here we go . . . .

As they were waiting for their cab to the airport Alan decided he wanted to barter with their cabby. Donna tried to tell him that the Mexicans know when they're leaving and there's a set fee to the airport. As Alan was arguing with the driver, he drove away while Alan was standing on the curb yelling obscenities and gesturing with his hands on his crotch.

"Yeah? Suck me off you black l'il fucker!" he screamed out loud at the top of his lungs.

Oh My God, she couldn't believe he did that. Donna was so embarrassed she had to walk away. He called her minutes later when the next cab arrived and they left for the airport.

They rode in silence and on the way; they witnessed a man get hit by a bus. The driver fled and no one stopped to help. Donna was horrified. There was this man and his bicycle on the side of the road while people just walked around his body as though he weren't there.

"How can we not help?" she asked.

"He's already dead, there's nothing we can do", Alan said.

As they were waiting in line to leave the country at the airport, Alan couldn't find his tourist card. No one leaves Mexico without a tourist card. Oh no, she thought, now what? Does she stay with Alan? What should she do? She started to panic. Alan desperately rummaged through his bags in front of everyone, as the guard watched suspiciously. The guard told them they could not leave the country without it. Only minutes before departure, he found sympathy and told them to go. Thank goodness, she thought, not only was Alan drunk, but he had also lost his tourist card.

Chapter 14

Their life after that became a roller coaster. Not because of Alan's drinking. That didn't seem to make a difference. He could be totally dry and he would still change personas. It was like he was two different people. It seemed crazy and it was hard to believe. He had been smoking pot throughout the relationship and she drank. Who was she to judge? His anger and loudness became unbearable. Everyone knew his thunderous laugh. It was extremely loud with a kind of hork to it. You could tell who it was anywhere. It was actually an embarrassment, as it always attracted attention. But Alan liked attention, no matter what kind.

Alan needed constant praise. People would comment to Donna how he could never walk past a mirror, without checking himself. He would arrive home agitated and never give a reason. She learned quickly to read his moods. Were his eyes large and piercing or relaxed and loving? They could change in an instant, anywhere, anytime. She began to walk on eggshells, nervously waiting to see what his frame of mind would be each day. It was in these times that Donna had to learn how to bite her tongue and stay silent. This was a huge challenge for her, since it was not her nature to remain silent. If anything, she spoke at the wrong times.

They went back to Winnipeg for a hockey tournament. Alan's hockey team was having a banquet and they were staying at Donna's friend Sherri's home. Donna invited her close friends to join them. It was to be a fun evening with friends from both cities and she was excited to go. As they were driving down the main road of the city, they stopped at a red light. They were chatting and as she turned to look out her window a young fellow smiled at her. She smiled back.

Alan became furious. "Why did you make eyes at that guy? What the fuck are you doing?" he screamed.

"I smiled back at a young kid," she said. "What was I supposed to do, give him the finger?"

Alan rambled on for the rest of the 20-minute drive. Was this to be a fun evening? She got out at the club and their friends joined them as they walked in. Sherri, Deb and Donna were walking when Alan suddenly whispered, "Whore" under his breath. She was certain that she had misunderstood him. Surely he wasn't calling her that name? Deb & Sherri gave her a strange look when Donna asked what he had said. Then she heard it again.

"Whore!"

She was absolutely crushed.

"Did he really say that" she asked?

"It sounded like he said whore." Sherri said

Oh my God—in front of my friends she thought. The night got worse from there. She kept her distance from Alan for the remainder of the night, since she wasn't quite sure what to expect. She mingled in the social circle of people they knew and pretended to enjoy the evening. As she chatted with some of Alan's co-workers they asked if he was behaving.

Donna then said "If I were a bigger person, I would like to punch him right in the mouth."

No one asked any more questions.

Alan was starting to feel remorse for what he had done. He was about to start the emotional blackmail by telling people Donna was angry with him in order to get sympathy. Sherri and Deb remained by her side the whole night. When the evening ended Donna didn't know what to do. She drove the car since Alan had been drinking and Sherri's house was five miles out of the city. Alan rambled the whole way there. Yelling, cursing and so very loud.

"What the fuck Donna! You come to a function of mine and then you don't even fucking talk to me. What a fucking bitch you are!" He screamed.

She finally yelled back "Stop this battle or we could get into an accident. I can't drive with you screaming at me."

They were midway between Winnipeg and Headingly on a very busy part of the Trans-Canada Highway. This stretch of highway was well known for car accidents. Donna stopped on the side of the highway and Alan got out of the car, she thought to cool off. He came around to her side and opened the door and he pulled her out of the car. There she was at 2:30am, standing on the highway in the middle of nowhere, while Alan drove off in her car. Donna had nothing with her. No money, no purse, nothing. She was sure he would turn around however he drove off until he was completely out of sight. As semis honked and cars drove by she tried to stay calm. It was on this very highway when she was fifteen that a girlfriend and her took a ride from a stranger. It was not a pleasant memory as this man, in a small red Toyota had no intentions of letting them out. As he held tightly onto her girlfriend's breast, Donna begged him to stop the car. Intuition took over. She opened the door, pulled her friend out and they landed on the roadside. Scraped and bleeding they ran to a service station only to meet a deranged hitchhiker who they told the story to.

"You'll be okay" he said. "I have a knife in my boot and I killed a man."

Oh Geez, she thought as she quickly convinced him they'd be back. They locked themselves in the bathroom at the service station until her friend's brother came to rescue them.

Donna thought of walking back to that very same service station this night, but would it be open at 2:30am? She chose to walk ahead since she knew there was a motel up ahead. The office would not answer. She was grateful to see a payphone outside. Donna had no money, so she called 911. Within three minutes three police cars arrived. She was thankful, embarrassed and humiliated that she actually had to call the police. They drove her to Sherri's where Alan had already gone to sleep. They woke him up, spoke to him and considered it alcohol related. They asked him to sleep it off. It was never mentioned again. If she tried to talk about it, Alan would get angry, only to say "it was over, in the past." "In the past", was a term which she was to hear often over the next few years.

* * *

Donna was seeing her friends less and less. Alan was always disappointed if he couldn't reach her at any given time. Oh how he loved her. She didn't feel the need to have her own time, her own friends and later, her own choices. Alan provided all of that. More and more he demanded to see Donna's will. In his frequent moments of anger, he would always bring up finances and her will. Over time she would re-write her will to put his mind at ease and stop the continuous battles. She worked hard to keep her home and she felt her children were the first priorities in her life. The girls were her responsibility and she had to make sure they were provided for should anything happen to her.

One day when Donna arrived home, Alan had a pen in his hand and figures sprawled all over his note pad. He was always so furious that she still had a mortgage on her home and other debts. He had told her how he could knock years off her mortgage if she put his name on the title. Donna was definitely not a financial wizard and everything he said made perfect sense to her. After all, he showed her his hand written prenuptial agreement clearly stating that this home was her future retirement fund as well as her daughters' education.

They signed the mortgage papers at the bank. The banker was a very nice woman who later became her client.

The banker kept asking "Are you sure"? A hint had gone unnoticed.

Chapter 15

*A*lan was becoming increasingly more demanding. Everything had to be in its place in the home. A cup left on the living room counter one evening when he returned home from work, sent him into a furious rage.

"Why the hell can't you pigs pick up after yourselves? You fucking sloths! Why don't you pigs go live at your trailer trash father's, who isn't even man enough to pay his child support!" he screamed.

Donna was absolutely appalled. The ranting went on for two days. Her youngest daughter took to spending long hours in her room. The outbursts worsened. She tried talking to Alan in a calm, mild manner.

"Alan I think we should take a break. I mean I can't seem to make you happy and it's stressful for both of us." She said.

He would then soften and at times break down in tears.

"But I love you so much Donna. I can make you a very happy woman. I'm so sorry; my job is so mentally grueling. I'll seek help for this violent illness of mine and I will recover, I promise." He said.

Then in the next hour after some time alone he would retaliate. It was absolutely crazy!

"I'm gonna fucking break you! I'm going to run you out of town and take fifty percent of your home and everything you own." He ranted.

Money became a frequent threat. His anger became unbearable. Alan worked shifts and it seemed as though his fits of rage always fell on his days off. He would keep her awake all night, calling her all his infamous words. She was forced to work in a state of exhaustion, too embarrassed to tell anyone why. How would anyone believe her after witnessing all the love he showered her with?

Donna's girlfriend Tanis had told their mutual friend Rita that Alan and Donna were a match made in heaven. She told Rita that she had spent an evening with them in their hot tub and that they were made for each other. Tanis praised them to no end. Rita found this hard to believe. She had worked in the area of abuse, and had Alan in a program, which she led. She was not to be fooled. Rita would become a lifeline for Donna later when she would feel Alan's wrath. She instilled a strength and hope in her.

Donna was so mentally and spiritually exhausted, that for days she simply did not want to wake up. She lay in bed, lost in loneliness and despair. Surely life had more to offer than this? She felt as though she could no longer be the mother that she wanted to be for her daughters. She knew she had instilled the most important qualities in her girls and that they knew she loved them. She told them often. She had become so very tired.

The words of a former employee often haunted her.

"He's a scary man. He's crazy. I have a friend who he stalked and she wants to know if you would like to read the letters he wrote her?" she asked.

Of course Donna didn't. This was a man she believed no one really knew. How right she was!

"Do you know about the waitress he stalked? He was barred from the lounge." The employee added.

Donna did not want to hear it. Even though she recalled Alan mentioning to her that if she joined him for drinks it would likely make a certain waitress jealous. She was not into games and made that very clear when he later decided to alter his story.

She was later told that this waitress's co-worker held a broken beer bottle up to his neck and said "If you ever fucking come near her again I'll slit your throat"!

Donna received numerous love letters from Alan. Such sweet words that touched her heart when she read them. Time and time again she would find forgiveness in her heart. She felt pity for this man and his misfortunes. Gifts would arrive at unexpected times for no reason. When she arrived home from work one day she found two new outfits that Alan had bought for her. Although they were not her style, nor color of choice, it was this loving gesture that allowed her to wear the clothing with pride. Donna received daily emails filled with loving words but she also received threatening abusive letters too. They would later be brought to light.

* * *

Alan and Donna were at George and Sheila's home when Rita, Tanis and Sheila commented on their shopping trip to New York. Donna had missed out on it. As they chatted and drank beer, she mentioned that they should all go to Mexico sometime. Alan became furious. His eyes began to bulge. He started to swear and rant about how she was not going to use his money! She had never used any of his money. He was on a downward spiral once again. He became uncontrollable and the crowd sat silent with all the women staring at her with fear on their faces. They left. Alan was extremely upset. As they were driving home, her cell phone rang. It was Alan's friend. It was the only friend she ever knew Alan to have. After a brief conversation, Alan hung up.

"What the fuck is he doing calling your cell? Are you fucking him Donna?" he screamed.

She tried to tell him that he must have given him her cell number. The proof came later from her daughter who said that Alan's friend had called and asked how to reach them. She had given him the number.

Donna started to confide in her staff. They were like sisters to her and Lina knew there was something seriously wrong. She mentioned some of the scenarios and Lina was completely dumbfounded. Up until this point she had only witnessed pleasant moments between Alan and Donna. But it was Lina who had the uncomfortable feeling about Alan in the very beginning.

Alan came home in an ugly mood once again. Donna had her cell phone on and held low in her hand when he started to rant. Nothing was good enough.

"Why do you always feed me fucking slop? You and your kids are the three fucking bitches from hell!" he yelled.

As she lifted the phone and acknowledged Lina, he was quite surprised but not nearly as surprised as Lina was.

"Oh my God, I can't believe that's Alan?" She said in shock. "This is not good, I can't believe this!"

Alan took the phone from her hand and started talking.

"Hi Lina, what seems to be the problem here?" he calmly asked.

After a few minutes he hung up and continued where he had left off. Most of the time, her daughters were out of earshot of these tirades. She realized she had to find a way out.

Donna was unfamiliar with the whole cycle of abuse. In a desperate moment and tired from never getting proper sleep, she found herself calling the crisis center. They asked her to come in to their office. She was exhausted and worn out. When she started to explain the situation, they asked her his name.

"Alan Harris," she said.

"Oh Alan, yes I'm very familiar with the man." the woman said nonchalantly.

Donna's heart sank. She was now part of this mad man that everyone seemed to know so well. The words of warning from her friends when she first met Alan were all coming back to haunt her like a deadly lurid nightmare.

She no longer cared if anyone believed her or of any of the consequences Alan had threatened her with. In his next fit, when she asked him to leave, he kicked her out of bed into the wall. He insisted it was his bed and he wanted her out. Not a rolling push where one lands on the floor, but a cannonball kick where she hit hard against the solid log wall. Donna had been seeing an orthopedic surgeon for a rotator cuff/shoulder problem and the blow to her right side was extremely painful. Anger overtook fear. She was now ferocious as she stood up and grabbed the boudoir lamp on her night table and hit Alan hard. No one was going to hurt her she thought.

"You fucking hit me!" he repeated a few times, talking in a violent psychotic voice.

"Yah and don't you ever fucking touch me again!" she screamed.

She was going to give back as good as she got!

Donna knew she was in trouble then. Alan walked to her side of the bed, grabbed her right arm and twisted it behind her back until she hit the floor hard. The pain was excruciating and she lay there while to catch her breath. It hurt beyond tears!

"Fucking bitch!" he ranted.

That was it! Donna called the police. Alan was removed from her home and a restraining order was placed against him. She was relieved and devastated all at the same time. How could this man who supposedly loved her so much, the only man who had ever been so attentive and caring, be so cruel and abusive? She was sick for days. Her Irritable Bowel Disease flared up and the bleeding and pain had become increasingly more frequent. She had difficulty sleeping and it became a challenge to eat.

Her friends both at work and outside of work were very supportive. Trying to console her and tell her how she could do so much better. It was little relief at the time but certainly the support and comfort she needed.

"Why doesn't she leave him?" is the often asked question about women who live in abusive relationships but for them, the question is more "How can I leave him?"

Many such women get hooked into the unreality of the dance of lies and broken promises that the abuser orchestrates. The highs are so high that they temporarily block out the lows. Donna believed that she had the best people in her life. It was these people who helped her to survive. They were her lifelines!

Chapter 16

*L*ina called in a desperate voice and asked if they could talk. Alan had contacted her and asked if he and Donna might talk. In her weakness she agreed. She was about to make another mistake! Alan convinced her that he was about to lose his job. He held a position of power and it was highly against the rules to have any dealings with the police. Alan was a peace officer himself. He told her how his whole future would be over and he begged her to call and have the order removed. She had never dealt with the police and the court system before but Alan seemed to know the system well. Donna worked hard all her life so how could she risk a hard working man's job? After all, they were going to get him help since he had admitted to having some serious problems.

She called the judge. He told her he wanted to ask her one thing and to think about it before she answered.

"Is anyone making you do this?" he carefully asked.

"No sir, I'm hoping that maybe now with my support, that this man might get the help he needs. He's asked for help and I'm willing to give it my best." she said confidently.

"OK, Best of luck to you", he said.

Donna thanked him and the order was removed. She had made a serious mistake!

Alan did go for help. He had previously been in men's Anger Management Program years before he met her. He re-joined his twelve-step program. Donna was to learn later that he had done so many times before to no avail.

Over time, nothing improved. Alan always commented that everyone they knew were alcoholics, whores, and sick in some way or another. Were all of these people so bad? She begged to differ. It was these same people who were to help her through all of this turmoil later on.

After many furious episodes, Alan agreed to try alternative naturopathic measures. Some of which Donna felt lessened the rages, but nevertheless they still continued. Alan seemed to be at his calmest, most tolerable moments, after he smoked a joint, she was to learn later. It was like a monthly PMS cycle. She dubbed it Pre-MENTAL syndrome. The episodes became weekly, then almost daily.

Alan was so proud of the fact that he had been totally faithful to her. Isn't that what people do when they love each other? She wondered. Donna couldn't understand why one would be so pleased with their fidelity. She assumed it was a normal part of any healthy relationship. When he was in angered moments, he would threaten to go find another woman. One of the many, which he claimed, that were waiting in line for him. Donna would later pray for any such woman to appear and rescue her from this hell.

Alan had agreed to go with her to see a Catholic Priest. Although she was not a practicing Catholic, Donna still had faith and hope. She told Father, word for word, in plain English what Alan had been saying and doing. He sat there with a dumbfounded look on his face. He remained speechless for several minutes.

Father asked Alan, "Do you really say and do these things?"

"Yes, it's what I do," Alan answered calmly with little expression.

"You need to pray" he suggested.

"I have been praying Father, it's not working" Donna said.

They left.

Alan was in a gentle affectionate frame of mind as he lay in bed. Donna pondered how this man could seem to be like two different people. The Alan she met was compassionate and kind with soft sparkling eyes and the other was angry, loud and foul with large piercing green eyes. She longed for the attentive gentle soul she knew was deep within him. Donna knew she could help him. She really believed with the right measures he could put all his anger aside. They could live a harmonious life and live the dreams they both shared. Suddenly Alan's eyes began to well up and she cautiously asked him what was wrong.

"I'm afraid that I might hurt you." He said in a soft caring voice.

"In what context do you mean? Physically or emotionally?" she asked.

"Both", he said.

Donna lay silent.

She went to talk to Alan's mother. She was desperately seeking some answers.

"Has he hurt you?" his mother asked.

"Not yet" she lied.

"Well he does have the capability to!" she said matter of factly. "Has he been using?" she asked.

Using what? How was she so knowledgeable about his lifestyle? Why had no one told her? They had. She chose NOT to listen.

Alan's parents had raised him in a pathetic drunken, drug-addicted environment. They were both clean and sober now.

"I can't live like this." Donna said.

"You don't have to." his mother said.

Donna told her about some of his anger episodes. His mother suggested she join Al-Anon to learn how to cope. Donna did not feel that was the answer for her. She did not want to learn how to cope with this violent abuse. She wanted it to simply end. She did go to Al-Anon. She quit drinking alcohol to assist in Alan's rehab. It did not help. She quit having any privacy at all. He preferred her to be available to him at all times and not spend time with friends alone. Nothing helped.

They were at Alan's folks for dinner. There seemed to be no boundaries for Alan's father. He ranted the same as his son. Obviously Alan had been raised in an environment where abuse and vulgarity were acceptable. She supposed it was similar to her own father's acceptance of the same.

Chapter 17

Summer found them going to the Alan's family island. How excited they all were at the thought of being on an island—fishing, boating, skiing and for Donna, tanning. In the beginning they called it paradise; however that name would soon change. There were stringent island rules. The children had to put in two hours of work every morning, starting at 7:00am in very high temperatures. Of course, they were being paid, so it was justified in the old man's eyes. As Alan's father sat in his chair, the king of the island demanded each child be assigned a chore of: raking, moving rocks, hauling garbage and moving deadfall. One of the kids was out of sight as the old man peered around; she was assigned another thirty minutes of work for being absent. She had gone to the outhouse. Donna watched as her daughter toiled in the heat as her cheeks turned redder by the moment. She realized then that this may not be the fun trip that they had anticipated. She asked that the kids have a rest period. Enough was enough.

Lina and her family also joined them in this first island excursion. The old man had set them up and they did have a good chuckle. Under his direction they were to take the first trail to their left and explore the island. This was an opportunity to sneak off for a beer so they were more than happy to go for the hike. Just as they were to turn on the next trail they came upon a grizzly bear in attack mode up on his hind legs with huge teeth viciously bared. They both screamed and of course Donna was the one to yell out the loudest obscenity. They had been set up. It was a prop, set up within tree branches. It never dawned on them for a moment that there were no grizzlies in this area of Canada. They sheepishly walked back to the cabin where the crowd was roaring with laughter.

Donna felt humiliated that Lina's sons had to work so hard every day, moving rocks in order to earn their keep, even though they brought all of their own provisions. Lina was an accomplished artist and had spent her days on the other side of the island, painting a huge rock with the "Harris" Family name on it as a gift in return for her stay. It was beautifully created and was placed on the large rock that led to the entrance of the island.

Donna was appalled at her first visit to the outhouse. Not because of the conditions, since Alan's mother made sure it was clean and comfortable. But by the mounds of smut magazines in the rack made her stomach churn. There were rather racy magazines with vividly graphic pictures of women in every possible pose. This in her opinion was unacceptable for young children to view. She mentioned this to Alan and after a day trip to town, they returned to find them all hidden.

The kids were too tired to do much of anything after their chores; however they did get to swim in the lake. Fishing was a joke. They were only allowed the boat on a designated day and it had a time limit. If it was a rainy day or too windy, too bad. The kids had asked for permission to use the plastic kayak for a few hours. The fun ended quickly as an oar sank to the bottom of the deep cold lake. There was no possible way to retrieve the oar in these deep waters. They had to spend the rest of the day looking through store catalogues to find a current price so that they could repay Alan's father. So much for the money they had earned.

The path across the island left the old man tired at the end of his walk. Donna decided to make him a willow bench out of the fallen trees on the island. She planned, measured and constructed it within a few days. She was pleased with the finished product and she was sure he would be surprised and pleased. How wrong she was once again! As they walked with Alan's dad down the path he suddenly noticed the new bench on the rock. There it was facing the sunset and the sunrise.

"I sure the hell hope you didn't cut too many of my trees down for Christ's sake!" he spewed.

She felt awful and let him know that in fact she used only fallen trees. No more was said.

Their every move was monitored by Alan's dad. He had made the island hell and it began to feel like Alcatraz. They had decided to go to a neighboring island where there was an actual beach. There were limited rules regarding safety and they could all feel free to laugh and frolic. Of course they had to beg permission to use the boat. The kids asked if next time they came if they could rent a cabin on this island which was so much fun. They boated home at sunset along the lakeshore. The skies were full of color and the scene was breathtaking. Earlier in the day, they had radioed the home island telling them not to hold supper, as they would enjoy the sun for the day. Donna jokingly radioed to "King of the Island" knowing that no one else on the radio would connect who it was referring to. She thought the old man would get a kick out of it. She certainly had no idea that there would be any issues with them spending the day away. When they walked into the cottage and announced their arrival, the old man was furious.

"Who the hell do you think you are? You and your damn kids!" He screamed.

His eyes were huge and his voice even bigger. His wife sat silent as Donna apologized three times as she struggled to hold back tears.

She didn't even know what she was apologizing for. Finally Alan jumped up and angrily approached his father.

"What the hell is wrong with you? First you abused mom, then my sister, and now Donna! I won't stand for your fucking bullshit! You're exactly like grandpa and I don't want to be anything like either of you sick bastards!" he screamed.

Donna began to tremble as she watched this nightmare unfold. They yelled obscenities at each other and she was terrified that they were going to hit each other. Alan's father was a miserable, overweight, heart diseased diabetic. She tried to hold Alan back. Alan wanted to leave the island but it was a five-mile boat ride, it was getting dark and the waves were getting high. She had a fear of water and begged him to leave in the morning. The old man left the cottage. Donna retreated to the bedroom while her daughters went out to the guest shack. They packed their things and woke up early and took one of the boats. They left quietly and docked it where they always docked. It was such a relief to be off of that island where conflict was constant.

They didn't see Alan's parents again for six months. When Donna eventually visited them, Alan's dad spoke up.

"I don't know what exactly I said when I saw you last but I do know why I said it. It's because I haven't been to an AA meeting for four months." he said.

What a weak feeble excuse, she thought to herself. No apology was made nor was one ever expected. There was no more discussion.

The same scenario presented itself again the following summer. The old man took it upon himself to move the kid's inner tube, which had been dragged up on shore and secured it with a rock as the winds were quickly approaching. The next day when he confronted one of the children about securing the tube she swore that she had secured it and was in disbelief that it was found in the bushes. She was so distraught and in tears, leaving doubt in everyone's minds as to what really happened. Donna spoke with her privately and knew something was not right. Alan later said that he, himself, had carried the rock for her in order to secure the tube. Alan confronted the old man and he admitted moving the tube himself. He said that he was teaching the children a lesson. What a lesson Donna thought, to be taught from a lie! It was a tube, which the kids had purchased by pooling their own money and they had been taking good care of it. She felt so sorry for Alan's soft-spoken mother. It was on this visit that his mother broke down and screamed back at the old man for his cruel ways. She insisted that it was her island as well. Donna was proud to see her stand her ground however she worried at the consequences her actions might bring. How could the old man justify his actions? Donna thought he was crazy! She chose never to return to "Spaz Island", as the kids had now dubbed it, ever again.

Chapter 18

A client, who was a mental health worker, had asked Donna out for coffee. They had discussed rather personal issues throughout the years and their admiration for each other was mutual. Donna would learn some extremely disturbing facts from the reading material that was given to her. Three different personality disorders showed a pattern of sexual deviancy. After their abusive fits, these types of people craved sexual release. Donna felt as though she was living a nightmare-this was her current life to a tee. She became more and more disturbed as she studied the medical pamphlets. After an episode of Alan screaming and yelling, he would always end up going into the bedroom. Donna walked in shortly after an episode, to confront him and suggest that nothing was helping this relationship. She was disgusted to find him masturbating and watching a porno video. He always claimed sexual frustration after his rages and he said that she should be there for him. Strange how in his loving moments it was a part of their relationship he constantly praised. Donna was disgusted with this way of thinking. It was as though his abusive behavior warranted a loving sexual encounter He repulsed her!

Alan began to obsess with the fact that she would not partake in anal sex. It simply was against her own personal preference and her mind would never be changed regarding this act. He seemingly accepted her choice, however in an unexpected moment he stormed into the kitchen.

"Why don't you let me fuck you up the ass Donna?" he screamed at her.

She was sickened at his ways. She would never ever agree.

Christmas was approaching and Donna's mom and papa were to arrive. She was always so happy to have her folks and this was always a wonderful time of the year for them. She had started the home cooking that the girls and her prepared every year. When they arrived, Donna was more than ready. Alan came home from work in a tiff. Surely he wouldn't blow up in front of her folks, she thought. She could feel the tension in the air and she knew that he was well on his way. Her folks became quiet and felt uncomfortable. Suddenly he was angry because her papa, mom and her were drinking a beer, reminiscing and enjoying their time together. It was a weekend and no one had to work, but they had started without his presence and his permission. His rants began.

"You're a selfish and inconsiderate bitch. You never think of me and how hard I work!" he yelled.

It got worse. He was uncontrollable and without any sensibility. He rambled on as her parents sat at the kitchen table, silent! Her father looked into space and her mother stared at the floor. Surely someone would say something. As his voice became intolerable, Donna finally screamed at him.

"Shut up!"

This was simply unacceptable. He left the house and drove off in a fury.

"This isn't good," papa said. "He isn't even making sense".

"He's going for help. His job is taking its toll on his nerves." Donna said.

Her papa was very concerned

"I'm not so sure that someone like that can even be helped." He said.

That night didn't end well. Alan returned even more enraged. The police were called and he was asked to leave. Donna was so embarrassed.

Her papa lived the rest of his days, fearful of what might happen to her children and her. Future calls would find him worried and asking her how things were. If she needed help he would be there anytime. She didn't need her elderly parents ten hours away; worrying about her. It was her own fault, and she would deal with it. If only it were that simple. Over the next week she was to receive numerous e-mails from Alan. In many, he was begging for forgiveness and once again expressing his love for her, telling her how much he needed her and how so very sorry he was. He wrote that he was, and could be, a good man. He begged for reconciliation. Donna was foolish enough once again to fall back into the very trap that she had desperately tried to get herself out of. She began to question her own sanity.

Chapter 19

They had purchased tickets to Hawaii a while before. The trips to exotic lands that Donna once enjoyed immensely would soon become places of doom. Once again thinking this break would do them nothing but good, they set off to Oahu. They stayed at a friend's house in Alberta until their flight the next day. Lana had mentioned how she wished her own husband would give her the attention that she saw Alan give to Donna. She told her how happy she was that Donna found a man that was so good to her. They never saw Lana together as a couple again.

Hawaii was as warm and fragrant as she remembered from her first hot vacation, which she took her mother on, to celebrate her 65th birthday many years ago. Donna's husband, who she had not yet married, had backed out of the trip. He didn't want to give up two weeks of snowmobiling. She remembered the romantic places and how she wished he were there with her to share them. Instead, she shared the sunsets and seafood dinners with her mom and sister-in-law. As they searched for her sister-in-law's long lost sister, she constantly ached for the man that chose to remain behind. She felt so lonely.

This winter escape would be different. Donna had Alan with her. And different it definitely was! The temperatures were scorching and she basked in the sun daily. She headed towards the ocean to cool off, while Alan remained on shore watching her every move. An 83 year old man had started a friendly conversation with her in the water. He and his wife had retired there and he had offered to show them the Island. Donna pointed out Alan as he lay on the beach and the man pointed out his wife. They agreed that they would all get together later but when she walked towards Alan she could see he was furious.

"Why the fuck do all the rich old men approach you Donna? "What the fuck were you talking about?" he asked sarcastically.

"For God's sake," she said. "He is 83. What do you think I'm going to do?"

Donna decided not to make eye contact with the man as he came out of the water. She kept her sunglasses on to shield whether or not she was sleeping. Alan sent an icy glare at the man and it was obvious he was unwelcome. She never saw the man again and that evening would become hell! Alan would not let the topic go and he continued harping on it for the next three days, making sure neither of them rested.

The third day Donna was emotionally exhausted and called home to her salon to talk to Lina. She didn't know what to do. She was in another country with a crazed partner. Lina was at a loss for words and Donna was regretful going on this trip. The next morning she grabbed a few things along with her beach bag while Alan was in the bathroom, and decided to head off in search of a quiet piece of beach in which she could catch up on sleep. She was familiar with Alan's sleep deprivation tactics and knew she would need to catch up on rest whenever she could. Donna took little relief in the solitude she found and began to drift in and out of consciousness. Suddenly there he was! Angry at the fact that it took him four hours to find her!

He was clearly exhausted as well and started to calm down. They decided to go to a local nightspot that they had heard about. It had country music, which was something Donna enjoyed. She had taken dance lessons many years ago, but Alan had never really learned.

They met some local people and Alan seemed to be in good spirits and having a lot of fun. One of the group asked if Donna could two-step when Alan told him she could and added that she was quite good at it. He suggested that the man and Donna be dance partners. They danced a two-step and continued with a swing dance. When the man asked if she knew another dance, Donna said yes. They continued on. Alan seemed to be approving, but apparently she had one dance too many. When they sat down it was clear for all to see that Alan was irate! He was upset because the man had his hand on her lower back. Donna wasn't sure where he expected his hand to be and tried to make light of it. She tried to explain in order for a man to lead, that he needed to press on his dance partner's back as he pulled the arm forward. This only infuriated Alan further. He decided they were leaving.

"Will you be ok?" a woman they met whispered in her ear.

"I'll be ok." Donna nodded with a smile.

They left. Alan walked way ahead of her as if he were abandoning a stray dog. She wished at that moment that she had been abandoned.

Chapter 20

*S*ummer time was her favorite time of the year, but summer with Alan was hell.

Once again gaining strength through her support system, she asked Alan for them to part ways. Donna simply felt as though she could never please him and the relationship was no longer one of any respect or unconditional love.

"Fuck you!" he yelled. "Remember Donna, I'll take you for everything I can get. I'll clean you out!"

Funny, she thought that she really didn't have much. Her home no longer mattered to her the way it once had. She had not had a decent night sleep in eleven days since Alan was on a long rampage. Every single day when he arrived home he was furious. Then he was on a six day-off stretch and Donna wondered how she was going to make it through. Alan would sleep during the day while she was at work and then keep her awake all night. She cancelled her day's appointments and arrived home unannounced. Alan was sound asleep. He would save his energy to torment her all night.

He refused to leave and after many days of sleep deprivation and his outbursts and threats the time had come. Donna had made arrangements to have him served legal papers. The letter was politely written requesting he leave the home until a third party was present to mediate.

It was a long weekend and she packed the camper, ready to go hide in the wilderness. Her children thought they were simply going camping. It was important to her that they knew nothing of the facts. Donna didn't want their young minds to worry or become as fearful as she was becoming. Then came a frightening moment. The server arrived an hour early! The blood inside her veins rushed and her heart began to pound faster, as she feared the scene that would follow. Alan didn't hear them as he was in the bathroom. Thank God! They left quietly and quickly. They knew of Alan from his history. They returned later and Alan was served on the deck early in the afternoon. His eyes bulged as he stared at Donna when she walked by. She drove off with the camper in tow. She felt very relieved and at the same time heartbroken.

Donna called her friends George and Sheila. They had witnessed some mood swings throughout the relationship. George had subtly suggested herbs and vitamins to Alan in a non-accusing manner one day, pretending not to know of Alan's anger. Sheila along with her mom, Pam drove up to the lake to comfort her. They stayed for hours as they sat around the fire. Both women could see Donna was very distraught and continued to talk with her about the situation. Donna had a difficult time keeping her composure constantly breaking into tears. The women left very late to drive back to the city. Donna had taken her cell phone and continuously checked her messages in case her parents had tried to reach her. It was Alan who had called numerous times. First he left loving messages, followed by ugly, angry threatening ones. Donna never returned any calls. She was safe in her camper in the forest where no one could find her. Surely he wouldn't show up here.

She returned three days later with Lina and her friend accompanying her. Alan had left, and the house was in shambles.

There were notes everywhere with terrible writings. There was writing on mirrors, hats, books, calendars and anywhere else one could think of. The words "fucking bitch" were written across a mirror. The mirror that Alan had repaired on her antique dresser was removed. On the birthday calendar he had viciously scratched out his family's names. Beside Donna's name the words "Fuck Off" were written in large letters. On his birthday where she had written Al, it now read, "FUCK OFF Its ALAN YOU FUCKIN LOSER".

Days later her children would come to her with another note they had found somewhere. He had gone through Donna's drawers and torn pages out of her journal from her days as a child. Many of her belongings were gone. Somehow it didn't matter. It was a small price to pay for the peace and quiet without Alan Harris. She was once again relieved and happy to sleep on the floor as he had even taken the bed. She could finally sleep. Just sleep.

Alan had shattered her Archangel Michael statue, which was on the dresser and had torn the dried white rose that hung on the wall with a poem that he had typed out for her. Was this ever going to end?

There were numerous orders placed against Alan over the next while. He even e-mailed Donna and asked her to attend court with him for support. She couldn't believe what he was thinking. He had no remorse, and she was unsure if he either couldn't remember what happened, or if he actually believed what he was saying and accusing her of. It was frightful. As soon as one order expired he would re-appear.

Donna came home late after a night at Rita's visiting, and as she was preparing for a peaceful night's sleep, she had a sense of uneasiness. She got out of bed, and opened her closet door. There he was—standing in her closet!

Please don't call the police!" he whispered.

She did, but he bolted and was gone again.

Somehow he managed to get into her house. He would hide under her bed, in her closets and would randomly appear anytime, anywhere. One morning as Donna awoke and went to look out her bedroom window at the morning sun in the forest—there he was, on her deck, staring right at her! How long had he been there? What would he have done, if there was someone else in her bed? Donna walked right onto the deck and felt as though she was losing her mind. How dare he? She shoved him and screamed out loud. She lost any of her fear and all 110 pounds of her was ready to fight. She was so beat and exhausted.

"Please Donna, please forgive me. I love you so much!" he said.

He left before she called the police.

Her fears became anger. Donna was ready to fight back.

At one point the RCMP had suggested that they try to get a mental assessment done on Alan. They had witnessed many of the incidents and one officer had recognized a similarity between the act Alan had committed and that of one of their own family member's that was very ill. For the moment Donna found some relief in the fact that someone had acknowledged the severity of the situation. The officer had contacted a Magistrate and a hearing was set up immediately. She had been woken up at a late hour and Donna was placed in front of her. She had ten minutes to explain the situation. She didn't have a clue where to begin. Donna tried to explain as much as she could, but she was scared and intimidated. The magistrate clearly told her that she would need more information in order to issue a request for an assessment. Donna felt humiliated and confused. It had not been her decision to be there, but she knew it was worth a try so why could the woman not see what was happening. Donna lost faith in the system. She knew just as so many other people had said, it always takes a tragedy before anything is done. This was like a scary movie and she was an unwilling cast member.

It would be some time later, in a moment of calmness, that Alan would admit to her that he had once been diagnosed as manic-depressive. He would later deny this saying that it was simply a ploy, to get out of work. Donna was desperately unhappy that the relationship was unsuccessful. She began to believe what Alan had said. Who would want her? She had two daughters, a large debt ratio and she was sick with a bowel disease. A disease that seemed under control until their relationship had become too nerve racking. Alan had drilled all of this into her so often that it became a part of her soul. She wasn't sure what to believe. He would make her pay and no one would believe her. But he was wrong!

Donna had confided in a few of her closest friends—even the most embarrassing facts. She held nothing back when she confided in Pam. Pam was older than her and was very level headed. One night, in a fit of rage, Alan had thrown Donna on the bed. He was angry because he wasn't receiving enough attention from "his wife", as he called her. He held her arms and sat on top of her. His strength was prevailing. Her head was hanging over the end of the bed and he proceeded to enter her mouth. It wasn't easy for him but it was less easy for Donna. He finished his act. She thought she was going to choke to death as her airways were being blocked. She survived . . . and he remained . . . unpunished.

Chapter 21

Donna's friends, Tanis, Rita and Sheila had planned a weekend trip out of town. They would take all their kids, rent a few hotel rooms and have a night out. Donna normally worked weekends but had booked off Saturday for the special occasion. She was excited about the getaway with her daughters and they were also looking forward to a day of shopping and waterslides. Friday they all decided to meet in a small local lounge for their final plans. Alan was out of the picture now, with an order to stay away from her home and herself so she had nothing to worry about.

The women enjoyed the evening and planned their weekend. While Donna was in the washroom, she ran into an old acquaintance and they started to chat. They must have been talking for about fifteen minutes, and then she returned to her seat. The owner of the lounge Janie, who happened to be a close friend of hers, approached her table to tell her someone had been looking for her. The women asked who it was but Janie didn't know. She didn't recognize him. Donna hadn't expected anyone and Tanis asked if it was Alan? Janie said that she didn't think so. He had very short spiky hair and no facial hair. She had many clients in her salon and many became friends. They never thought anymore of it.

Alan was a master of disguise. Whenever he was in trouble and started a new life, he would change his facial hair and alter his appearance. He had learned well and had developed quite a talent in this area.

They had all been having drinks and Donna chose to call the Designated Driver service where they drive you and your car home. As they were driving down the lane, she could see her oldest daughter, a teen, on the computer, on the Internet no doubt, she gathered.

She walked in the lower door up the stairs and into the kitchen. Suddenly her heart was in her throat, and she began to tremble as the chills ran up her arms.

"Wanna have another beer Donna? You stupid bitch. You leave your kids home alone and you have to work in the morning and you're out till midnight? I should call the police and report you, you fucking bitch!" he ranted with wild eyes.

She picked up the phone but the line was being used for the Internet.

"My word against yours you stupid fucking bitch," he said in a scratchy rough voice.

Donna had her cell in hand and pressed the recall button. Alan ran out the door. She took after him as she spoke to Lina on the other line. Lina begged her to turn back but Donna had enough and was willing to take whatever was brought her way.

The trees brought total darkness to the long lane way, as she pursued Alan. She asked Lina to listen and if anything happened to call the police. She had enough, and this was going to end. The only sound she could hear was herself gasping for air as she ran to find him all the while yelling at the top of her lungs.

"Ok, big tough guy, come on, you piece of shit", she yelled. "Well come on, why are you running if you're so tough?" she screamed. (Coward she thought)

Donna no longer cared what the cost was. She wanted this to end once and for all. She would have been in serious trouble had he decided to stop. He could have undoubtedly overpowered her but in that furious moment, she didn't care. She wanted her life back. She was tired of always wondering when and where he would be.

The leaves crunched beneath her feet. Donna couldn't find him anywhere. He had hidden his car and the trails through the forest were endless. She ran back to get her car. She had lost him. She had no proof. Lina had not heard his voice. Earlier Alan had called on his cell from the driveway and asked Donna's daughter to let him in. He told her they were meeting here. She had no idea of anything that was taking place that night. He had always tried to play her so she would side with him. She was a smart girl and soon realized his game. Donna did not want the kids involved ever.

She was totally exhausted in the morning since she had stayed awake all night. Donna wanted to cancel out on the weekend. Her stomach burned, her mind was weak and she had lost her strength. Rita and Sheila convinced her that she should sleep at the hotel. It would be better to stay away from her home.

Donna had 11 messages on her phone from Alan when she returned home:

- January 13th—6:43PM, 6:44PM-10:30PM in one to two minute intervals

His voice was twisted and threatening. She had him taped. She had evidence and lots of it. When her friends listened, they were all in shock.

- "Hey Donna, You Stupid Fucking Bitch!" "You're out all night, well you're gonna pay Donna", he eerily whispered in a raspy demon like voice.
- "And you know what else Donna? You're gonna pay . . . big time!" he seethed.
- I'm gonna run you out of town you stupid, Stupid Fucking Bitch", he ranted.
- "I'm gonna charge you with assault!" he threatened furiously.
- "And . . . you know what else Donna? I'm going to charge you with assaulting your children too!" he spewed.

Rita insisted these psychotic messages be taken directly to the police. Donna was too afraid of the threats. She feared what Alan would do if he lost his job. She kept the tapes. She was unable to comprehend that this man could and would do just about anything.

The young, female RCMP Constable would not give up on Donna, she was adamant that the circumstances that Donna found herself in were NOT to be taken lightly. After her insistence Donna started documenting everything-letters, emails, disciplinary actions, everything! The Constable was constantly telling her that this situation was one that could end in suicide, homicide or both! Donna could not even fathom the fact that she was in this situation.

How could she bring herself to watch another human being suffer? He was obviously in need of love, attention and her forgiveness. After everything he put her through, why would she even consider looking at him, let alone, take him back into her life again? Donna didn't understand, she had no answers . . . this must be how battered women feel, when they just can't figure out a way to escape. She wanted to be loved and he loved her-like she had never experienced before. He loved her, but it came with a price—would that price eventually be her life?

Chapter 22

They were at her mom and papa's for a vacation, Alan, the kids and her. Her folks lived in a resort Park, in a small cottage that papa built. Her girls had spent most of their summers there where the grass and flowers were abundant. The river was close to the house and it was their own little paradise. Donna and her papa would garden and drink beer while her mom complained that they were outside too much. Papa and Donna would chuckle to each other as they snuck another beer.

They loved summer and this time together was the ultimate pleasure for all of them. The girls would jump off the low river bridge and float over the mild rapids. Their laughter could be heard all the way downstream. This was the same park Donna went to when she was a child. The few memories she had of both her brothers being together. She remembered the teens on the dance platform as they played the jukebox while she hid under the open floor stage. Bonfires everywhere and her mom and uncle always playing their accordions, lots of music and dancing.

It seemed to Donna that in those days in that park, everyone was always happy. Just like papa brought happiness to her children. There was always a tube for floating, a tractor for towing and the night always ended with all of them roasting marshmallows on the flames of the open fire. These were fond memories not only for her, but also for her girls. Often they would stay longer than planned. They never wanted the summers to end since they met many friends in the park and fun was endless.

Papa wasn't feeling well. He had never complained before. Alan drove him to the doctor without anyone knowing—a kind gesture on his part that Donna could not disallow. Papa needed an angiogram and the test results later showed that he needed angioplasty.

The angioplasty was unsuccessful. Her strong, physically fit papa needed a heart bypass. She would be there just as he always was there for her. Her papa was so worried about Alan. They had agreed to put papa's name on her mortgage to cover any possibility of losing her home as Alan often threatened. It was a relief to know that papa and her had a plan in place.

The relationship with Alan simply was not working, Donna begged for him to get on with his life, but he refused to listen. After returning home from their summer resort, Alan was served on September 1st with an order to leave, giving him until September 3rd to vacate the premises and obtain a lawyer, failure to do so, would result in a restraining order being issued against him once again. She drove, and flew home as often as she could from September through to Christmas to help drive her mom to the hospital and be there for her papa. She was tired and worried. How could she make these trips, run her salon and tend to her daughters? Previously, Alan stayed with her girls when she went home. Now he was out once again.

Papa's bypass was grueling. He needed a quadruple heart bypass and lost a lot of blood. Donna watched the blood pour out as quickly as they were putting it in. He had many transfusions over the next few days. He was a tough old bugger. Days later she drove to the

City Hospital. Papa was coming home. She left her mom at the cottage. On the way home they joked about the whole operation. Papa told her they had one stop to make.

"No way papa, mom will kill me!" she said

"She needn't know," he said.

So she drove her papa to the small town hotel where the old folks often met. Heads certainly did turn, as her admired papa walked in, straight over to the VLT's where he could drop in $20. A few of the older folks that were in there greeted him openly.

"Get a beer," he ordered.

She did as she was told, they shared a beer and then she took him home.

Papa struggled, but did considerably well for such a surgery. He snuck in another beer the next day, and a few days later, she left for home.

How was she going to get out of the mess she was in? As soon as one restraining order was expired, Alan was right back in the house! She had to constantly stay on top of the expirations, but this was difficult to do as she was so concerned about papa's health.

She called Papa every day. He had follow up appointments with more bad news. Papa had cancer—prostate, testicular and colon cancer. He would have to wait until the six-month mark before his heart would be strong enough. But complications arose and his colon had to be looked after sooner than they hoped.

Papa's surgery was scheduled for December 15th. First however, they would take him in for the testicles to be removed. It took calls to four hospitals in and around the city to get him in on such short notice, as there was such a long waiting list for these types of surgeries. Donna called and spoke to him daily in the hospital.

She asked papa if he wanted her there for the next surgery or for Christmas. He insisted on Christmas because by then, he would be ready to come home.

Donna and her girls bought him a singing fish for Christmas. They knew he would love the tune of "Take Me to the River". Donna had attempted canvas painting the Christmas before under papa's daily and annoying guidance. The art turned out fairly well and of course Papa liked it. She decided while waiting for news about Papa, that she would paint his Christmas gift. She had decided to paint an angel walking the winding stairway to heaven with two young angels sitting on a nearby cloud watching the ascent. The colors were soft with glints of gold. She knew he would love it.

Chapter 23

*P*apa had been sick since summer and with Christmas approaching, she begged Alan to get on with his life. She tried to sleep in the guestroom, but he would bang on the door. If she slept in their bed, he would natter all night. If she would go to the couch, he would come and push her off. He demanded sex, but she would not give in. He was infuriated and ugly. If she gave in it only got worse. Donna was exhausted at work every day. Clients questioned her and she explained that she was worried about her papa. Some clients later admitted that they thought she was ill and hiding the fact. Well the truth was, she was hiding the living hell she was in.

Some of Alan's co-workers came to see her at separate times. They knew Donna was struggling as Alan was reprimanded at work and everyone knew his history.

"Do you know about the rape?" one man asked.

"Yes", she said.

In truth Donna knew nothing. She simply wanted Alan out of her life. She had stories of her own about him. People had mentioned, "The Rape" to her four times previously. What was this about? Who was raped?

She had nothing to lose, so she asked "Tell me about the rape?"

"I wasn't raped! What the hell are you talking about?" Alan yelled.

She had not suggested that he had been. She wondered just who it was that was raped. It came up far too many times. At times she wondered if "The Rape" meant he had been raped, or had he raped someone else? This was an incident that many co-workers claimed was the reason for his behavior, along with his crazy upbringing! Below is an excerpt form an article in the local paper:—It was alleged that Alan was one of the two staff members, and the actual details of what they endured during those twenty-two hours were never fully disclosed.

> "In March 1991, three inmates took two staff members and one inmate hostage for over twenty-two hours. The incident ended when members of the Emergency Response Team shot and killed two of the three hostage takers."

Donna had not had a decent night sleep in eleven days since Alan was on a long rampage. Every single day when he arrived home he was furious. Then he was on a six day off stretch and she wondered how she was going to make it through. Alan would sleep during the day while she was at work and then keep her awake all night. She was exhausted. She cancelled her day off at the salon and arrived home unannounced to try to get some sleep. Alan was there sound asleep resting up for his night of torment.

Alan called her his usual names. There was no reasoning. This life made absolutely no sense. It was her fault that Alan was frustrated.

She was to blame because the relationship was failing. Her parents were drunks, her kids were deviants, her friends were whores, her house was a mess, she owed debts and she was incompetent in every respect. Why then would he not leave? Why torture both of them?

Alan started to get very loud, knocking things around. Then he became downright ugly. He chased her into the kitchen. He had chased her throughout the entire house.

"Get back into the bedroom where a wife belongs!" he demanded.

As she ran in circles and back though the kitchen, Donna grabbed a knife. Alan stopped instantly. He was terrified of knives and she knew he would cower.

"Give me back the diamond ring that I gave you!" he screamed.

"I'll give you back the damn ring once and for all when I'm damn good and ready!" she yelled.

Donna had heard enough! She was ready to stand her ground and not give in to any more demands. That feisty attitude just added fuel to the fire. The staff had called from the salon and Alan didn't realize the phone had not been hung up properly when he took it from her hands. As Alan's anger exploded, he became more physical, pressing her up against the corner of the kitchen counter. She managed to slither out of his grip.

The chase was on and as Donna ran he called her every vulgar obscenity he could think of. She tried to reach a doorway, but found herself running in circles again. He caught her and wasted no time in twisting her hand and finger until the swelling would no longer allow the ring to budge.

"You're hurting me!" she screamed. "My finger is going to break!"

She finally broke down in tears and begged him to stop as she fell to the floor.

The girls on the phone heard it all. They had clients at the time, but took turns listening to the struggle. After what seemed an eternity, they called the police. The police arrived but Alan had fled. Donna expected him to threaten his usual, "her word against his". However this time, there was evidence. The police photographed her hand. It reminded her of a disheartening movie.—Only she was one of the main characters, this was really her life. December 20th, Alan was removed by the RCMP he plead guilty to assault, and was charged. The charges would eventually become a conditional discharge but kept on record in order to save his job. One more time . . . Unpunished.

On December 22, completely exhausted from the past eleven days with little sleep, she drove home to see papa for Christmas. The ten hour drive was far too much in her exhausted frame of mind. Her daughter offered to assist and Donna knew she couldn't argue. As she drifted off, occasionally opening one eye, she noticed they were in the wrong lane with a car fast approaching them. She yelled and grabbed the wheel. Her daughter was also falling asleep. Donna drove the rest of the way, only now she had turned up the volume on the radio to keep her alert. They arrived safely at her mom's house, but totally exhausted.

December 23rd Donna drove to Selkirk from her mom's house to see her papa. He looked very weak but he was quite alert. The girls had decided that they would walk in the room and tell him they needed him home. Donna eagerly agreed. When they entered, papa lifted his hands. Each girl took a hand, but could not speak. Their eyes welled up and neither girl said a word as they stared up at the ceiling. Papa squeezed their hands and told them it was going to be ok. Her heart bled for her young daughters as she could see the pain in their eyes for her brave adoring papa.

Her sister-in law came over to her mom's to visit that night. Alice was one family member who seemed to be somewhat consistent in her visits. Donna tried to explain the scenes that were taking place in her home. She had written a few pages in the journal that the RCMP recommended and handed it to Alice to read since she did not have the strength to explain what was happening in her life.

Alice's eyes began to overflow with tears before she broke down into a full sob.

Donna's mom simply replied, "Oh Well," with little expression.

Donna had hoped for more of a comforting response. She realized that her mother had other things on her mind. Surely she, who had been in a violent abusive marriage, would have more words of wisdom. She must have some answers for her own daughter. Donna needed her encouragement. She did not realize until then that Alan and her mother had been in contact with each other. They continued their relationship and her mother seemed to have received twisted versions of the actual truth.

December 24th Donna and her papa had a heart-to-heart talk.

"I'm worried about your mom" he said.

"She is the least of our worries right now, I need you to get better and come home. We have work to do." She said.

"I don't know if or when, or even why, they would send me home. They cut my balls off, removed my ass and there's nothing left." He said numbly.

She was surprised to hear her papa talk like that,—surprising words from man that never discussed sex or body parts.

They had made previous arrangements for her folks to move in with her. They spent winters with her and both loved the outdoor hot tub and it soothed their arthritis. Donna's staff loved her papa's daily visits and constant humor always waiting for the joke of the day. Her mom and papa had always taken care of the girls and the acreage so Donna could go away every winter for a break.

Papa started to talk about Alan.

"I think he's a very sick man. I'm worried about you." he said.

"I'll be fine papa." she said

"I hope so."

She didn't want to worry him anymore. It was late and her papa was tired. She kissed him and held him for a bit. She went home to her mom's. Donna planned to return in the morning with papa's gifts. She was anxious to give him the fish and the painting.

December 25th, 12:50am. The phone rang. Papa wasn't doing well; they had better get back there, the nurse said. The girls did not want to go back to the hospital, it made them feel sick.

Donna drove extremely fast to that next town and the lights flashing behind her were not going to stop her. Finally she thought with a police escort she would get there quicker, so she stopped the car quickly, jumped out and ran towards the police car that had been following her. He screeched in reverse, stopped his car and pulled out his gun. She told him her dad was dying and he led the way.

1:10 am. As she ran off the elevator towards the room, she recognized "that smell." Earlier that day as she was about to kiss him, papa suggested she not get too close.

"Why?" she asked.

"That smell," he said.

She realized later it was the smell of death he spoke of.

Papa was now pain free. He died at 1:00am Christmas morning.

Donna entered the room, absorbing the peacefulness. She ran her hand over her papa's forehead and brushed her fingers through his hair. She wept. Life would be forever changed without her papa. He was the one man in her life that left her only with pleasant memories. Her heart warmed with every thought of him. He never got to see his fish or the painted Angel. Her Angel, her Papa.

Christmas would never be the same. She followed through and prepared the complete Christmas meal. Tradition needed to continue as if papa was still there with them.

Her mother had changed her mind about everything they had discussed and agreed upon. Papa, mom and Donna had set the plan for her mom to move to Donna's home if anything should happen to him. Just as if he got well, they would move to her home together. Her mother was grieving and very angry. Donna left to go back to her home on New Year's Day. She had to tend to her business and get on with her life. She told her mom that she would be back at Easter.

Donna carried on with life, her daughters and her business. She thought of her papa every single day. The main man of her life was gone. How was she going to cope without him? Life goes on she kept telling herself. He would want her to be strong. So she was.

She drove the 500 miles to her mom's house with her daughters to prepare Easter dinner, but it was not a pleasant visit. They found her mother consuming huge amounts of vodka along with sleeping pills, antihistamines and extra strength Tylenol. Donna's youngest daughter took it upon herself to replace a bottle of vodka with water and Donna's mom never noticed the difference. Although it was sad, they chose to find humor in it. It was either laugh or cry. They chuckled as they watched her sneak water into her glass. Her mom's daily routine became twisted with her nights. She was demanding at strange hours and developed a strong bitterness towards Donna. She demanded that Donna stay longer and said that Donna should move back home with her. Once again Donna felt as though she could not please someone close to her heart.

When they left to return to their home, Donna's mom was angry! She chose not to look at Donna or to say goodbye. Donna's heart ached. She needed her mother. She felt she had failed her, and their lives for the moment had become strained. Her mom quit answering the phone and quit calling. She had disconnected the call display that Donna bought for her phone. Papa's friends would call Donna and keep her posted on her mom's happenings. She began to despise the calls even though they meant well, it was never pleasant news. Mom lost contact and the friends quit calling.

Chapter 24

Alan called her and tried another tactic. He was certain that she would never refuse a trip to Mexico. This time he couldn't be more wrong. What was it he did not understand? Nothing could change the way Donna had come to feel about him. She wanted him out of her life. He asked her a few times and then decided to take his daughter on the trip.

Donna received an e-mail from an unknown address. Being quite aware of viruses, she hesitated at first, but curiosity overtook her and she clicked to open.

> "HEY DONNA, THERE IS NO OTHER SOLE LIEKYOU! I MISS YOU WITH ALL MY HEART! I SAW TWO SETS OF FOOTPRINTS AND NO ONE BESIDE ME! I LOVE YOU! I MISS HOLDING HANDS, WALKING WITH YOU KISSING YOU, BEING WITH YOU, COMING HOME TO YOU. NUMBER ONE RULE FOR ALAN IS DON'T GET ANGRY WHEN MY PARTNER DOES SOMETHING I DON'T LIKE!" I LOVE YOU Donna XOXOXOXOX ALAN"

Alan added his usual sexual content as well. It sickened her to think he was so far away and took the time to find a cyber café in order to continue contact, even though there was still a restraining order in place.

Spring had arrived and Donna had made a personal commitment to have a pleasant summer. She had decided to redecorate the small camper that papa had given to the girls and her. She would paint the interior and replace the linoleum. She had always been a handywoman as her papa taught her how to survive on their acreage. Her youngest daughter would sew new curtains and it was all falling into place. This summer was going to be pleasant.

One night on the May long weekend Donna was removing the rest of the linoleum. Her cell rang, it was Alan. He wanted to know if he could come and get some of his things from the garage. She told him he could, but that he could not stay long.

She could not understand why he had asked to store his things in the garage. It was the least she could do he told her. It would save him the expense of paying for storage. But why didn't he simply come and get his things? It was something that he could contact her for. Alan had nice furnishings; however he had taken it upon himself, as broke as he claimed to be, to purchase new things. He bought a green leather sofa set along with a new DVD player and a new TV. Strangely enough, she had always said when she could afford it that she was going to buy a green leather sofa set. Alan already had a large TV in the garage when he purchased another one.

When he arrived at her acreage, he noticed Donna in the camper and stepped inside. She was struggling to remove some of the rivets along the edges of the floor. He offered to do the work and she accepted. He was civil and not the least bit nasty.

Alan wasn't there very long before she was called into the house and it sounded urgent. As she took the call, her heart sank. It was a client who lived close to the Salon

"Your salon is on fire!" she said anxiously.

Donna jumped into her car and Alan wanted to come with her. She insisted he take his own car.

When she approached the city, she could see the lit sky. The street was blocked off and Donna ran from her car towards her salon. Crowds of people were everywhere. Her business of seventeen years, her income, the building where her babies slept as the salon was constructed. Her work. What was happening to her world? Why? How? Who? She fell to her knees and became a broken woman. A shell of a human slowly crumbling.

Lina was there and Donna was becoming hysterical. Sandra and Janet had always tanned in the evening when all the salon activity was over for the day. Sandra had mentioned that she had planned to tan around 10:00pm. Where was she? It was 10:50? Please God, don't let this happen! Where's Janet?

As the fire roared and explosions kept erupting, she sat on the curb hanging onto her friend Darcy's legs. Begging for some miracle to stop all this pain. Her daughters immediately came to her mind. She realized both were safe, up at the lake with friends. It was then her cell phone rang. She was numb but relieved to hear her youngest daughter's voice.

"Mom, where are you?" she asked. "Mom?" she repeated, not knowing how to tell her she had just watched the fire on TV.

"I'm at the salon, watching the rest of it waste away before my eyes." She said. "There's no reason to come home there's nothing we can do. It's all gone."

Donna tried to call her other daughter, but she was out and about at the lake with her friends. When she finally reached her in the morning, her daughter was silent, not knowing what to say. The girls knew how she loved her business and the history those four walls held. Donna had a part of this place imbedded in her soul. Many of her clients became her friends. Some people became like family and she looked forward to their visits. She always joked that they were Psy-cosmotologists. People divulged their innermost secrets, just as she had exchanged with some of them. Her oldest daughter was to hear about the fire all the next day, as the teens gathered on the boardwalk at the lake.

Then Sandra arrived and they embraced as though they were long lost sisters, followed by Janet. Thank you God! Donna wept openly ready to give in to all. She was so very tired.

Alan was standing behind her and she was aware of his hand on her shoulder. She did not want his closeness even at this trying time. Donna's friends knew she was vulnerable in this weak moment, but she was very much aware. Alan had cried wolf once too many times. It would not work anymore. They all gathered at Lina's where they drank everything in sight. Somehow it didn't numb the pain. Her friends Janie and Rob even made liquor run to their lounge. Nobody slept.

The staff had already made up their minds. They were a team, and they were remaining a team, a sisterhood that she had always been grateful for. It was then she learned that she was blessed with wonderful people in her life.

It was believed children playing with matches started the fire; however no formal charges were ever laid.

Alan would later comment to her; "Thank goodness you allowed me out to the acreage last night to get my things. Can you imagine who people would have pointed the finger at"?

Chapter 25

George, Sheila and other friends had started to plan their annual summer event. They would all go for a night to their cottage and then on to the festival, which they attended every year. Alan knew very well the time and date as it was repeatedly advertised on the radio.

Trailer in tow, Donna and the girls headed to the lake full of excitement for the festivities ahead. They always brought along their own tents and they all had their own space. She was not happy when Alan appeared at the cottage. She thought George and Sheila had invited him and apparently they thought she had. Therefore they watched Donna strangely and she found herself a tad ticked off at them but kept silent.

This was a weekend where they really cut loose. They were all business people and it was their great escape. The lake was very quiet and remote where the cry of the loons was a soothing sound. She always looked forward to George and Sheila's hospitality in a completely relaxed environment.

The festival was a well-known family event where there was never any trouble. They really indulged at the cabin. It is safe to say that Donna clearly overindulged and decided to bid all a goodnight. She was lying in bed in her camper; her daughters were sleeping in the cabin. There was no indoor lock and Alan entered the camper. He was very quiet and she was almost in sleep mode however, still conscious. She felt the warmth of his breath on her back. She lay still. Maybe he'll go away if she doesn't respond she thought. He didn't. Then suddenly she felt him trying to enter her, from behind. Donna screamed as he attempted and he said he wouldn't hurt her. She put her hand behind her back, grabbed his penis and bent it hard. He backed off. She wished later that she had screamed louder and that she had made a scene.

The next day Alan followed her everywhere, even followed her to the bathroom. He asked her to hold his hand and that's when she finally exploded:

"If you ever try to come near her again I'll make sure you are put in jail." she spewed.

He asked her to calm down and she walked away. She hated him with all of her soul. Once again his deviant actions went . . . Unpunished.

Three days after another restraining order expired, Alan once again appeared out at her acreage. He was enraged with his bulging green eyes as he began to rant on and on.

"I'm fucking moving back in . . . tomorrow!" he threatened.

"I don't recommend it." she stated strongly. "Why would you want to be somewhere that you're not wanted?" she asked.

He was totally unreasonable and nothing she said would connect.

"Give me back the diamond ring!" he yelled.

"No problem! Make sure that you keep it this time!" she yelled back.

Donna had tried to return the ring many times before only to find it dangling on her car door, hanging on a tree branch, on the deck table or any other place he knew she would find it. She went into the house to get the ring. As she handed it to him, he demanded the diamond heart necklace and the diamond initial D that her daughters and he had given her for Mother's Day. She didn't argue. Whatever it took to get Alan Harris out of her life would never be too high a price to pay. He raised his arms as she stood there emotionless and he removed the necklace from around her neck. She later found the initial D on the outdoor table beside the fire pit. She wasn't surprised.

Alan left the acreage and as Donna continued on in her garden, she remembered how careless he had been with the full carat diamond ring. One would be certain to guard such a costly item with a little more caution, she thought. But then, why would he? She learned later that she was just as responsible for the payments on that ring as he was. Alan had purchased it on an extended line of credit attached to the mortgage on her home. He had maxed out the credit limit unbeknownst to her. She had never used that account herself and she was to end up responsible for half of that debt. In reality, she had been paying for her own ring. She began to wonder why the heart necklace that Alan gave her had been engraved with "Oui Precious, Love Alan". It was neither an expression he used, nor a name he called her. Perhaps this had been recycled, just as the dress he gifted her with might have been.

When she went in for a glass of water she noticed a message from her temporary salon location which she had constructed after the fire. She called to find the staff traumatized. Alan had just left there. He entered the Salon asking where the little tramp was. He proceeded to walk over to one of the girls as she was working with a client.

"There you are you little tramp." He said. He rambled a bit and then he walked out

125

Donna insisted they call the City Police. She would call the RCMP, which covered her acreage. She was not prepared to take any more crap from this man.

At that moment as she looked out the kitchen window, Alan was back. He went into the garage up on the hill and was carrying a gunnysack. She wondered what he was taking. Then she saw the chain saw. What the hell was he planning to do with that? She called the RCMP.

It took them a while to find him. He avoided going home to the suite he was renting.

"Is this was the same Alan Harris that lived in Greenwood Apartments?" the young constable asked.

"Yes" she answered.

"Oh yes, we know this guy and we will go talk to him." He said.

Donna was surprised at his comment since Alan had not lived there for quite a few years. Both police services warned him and another episode went . . . Unpunished.

Some days later Alan called, once again in a calm mood. He wanted some more of his things. When he came out, she asked him to finally take it all or she would have to remove it to storage. At this time she told him to be careful on his way out since there was a tree about to fall and it was likely to fall across the laneway. Donna watched and felt relief as she saw Alan drive away. He promised to remove his things soon. It was sometime later that he returned, claiming that he would have to stay since the tree fell and he could not leave.

Donna headed out down the lane. That tree was still above car height and it was obvious to her that someone had tried to fall it across the lane. However, it was caught in the V of another tree, which prevented it from hitting the ground. She told Alan that she knew he tried to knock down the tree.

He was upset at her accusation but she knew that damn tree was forced. It took him a while to leave and his vehicle was still quite able to drive underneath the fallen tree. She was perturbed that he would take these steps, but nothing surprised her when it came to Alan Harris. He had a new bag of tricks every week.

Chapter 26

With Alan finally out of her life, her house settled and his things finally gone, Donna began to live life again. Although she still found it difficult to go out publicly for fear of running into him, she had managed to join friends on occasion to attend different functions.

Donna no longer felt demoralized. She no longer took sick days off work. She had a huge support system with many people refusing to let her become a recluse. She took comfort living on her secluded acreage. She had two beautiful daughters who were the loves of her life. She had come to terms with many of the fears caused by the past abuse. Always being labeled as feisty and strong she vowed never to lose sleep again! She realized that Alan's threats were simply that, threats. She was not going to lose her home. Even though he threatened that he was going to charge her with assault, the facts would prove otherwise. Even when he e-mailed her changing one phony assault accusation to three, it didn't phase her. She could see he was inventing new stories, but she no longer cared. Donna had the best weapon of all, she had hope. She was finally free! He was gone. Still . . . unpunished!

Months went by . . . . Peace! Sleep! Calm!

As Donna opened the envelope and the pictures fell to her lap . . . she realized he was back. Not in sight but he was going to continue his abuse in another form. He must have taken some time to carefully remove her out of every photo. He removed himself from one in which they were walking along the ocean and wrote the name of her friend on the back. Craig was a friend from her hometown and Alan had never met him. He later quoted her mother, who had mentioned that she visited with Craig and his sister Betty. The contact between Alan and her mom continued. He had admitted this in another e-mail, which she printed off and kept. This letter did not need a return address; she knew damn well who had sent it once the photos fell out. Her full name was jaggedly written as though with a vibrating pen and an unsteady hand. At first she thought it maybe from her mother.

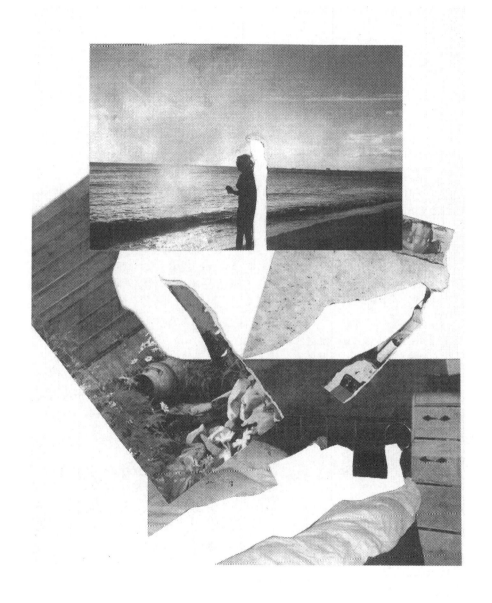

She had not expected any more contact and then the next day, Alan called her house leaving a demanding message.

"Pick up the phone or call me back!"

She did not respond.

The next message said, "We have unfinished business!"

He called again. This time the message sounded as though he were reading it.

"I want monetary compensation for the good I brought into your life. I *will* take you and my ex-wife back to court!"

Well at least he had a sense of humor Donna thought to herself as she chuckled. The following day as her daughter and she entered the lower level of their home she noticed a bottle of wine on the stairwell.

"I wonder where that came from." Donna said sarcastically.

Knowing very well who had likely left it there. Along with a nasty three page letter that Alan had decided not to sign. She had heard these words before, in the last message on her phone. He had been reading his own letter.

His closing words were, "You'll never hear from me again."

He lied! He continued to call her cell the following day. These next messages were different. Alan was desperate and crying. He asked to see her for just one minute and admitted that he was a pathetic mess!

Donna had learned from experience, never to trust Alan's words. She was a lot stronger at this point in her life and with the thoughts of papa's words of encouragement; she realized Alan wasn't powerful enough to break her. She had found her spirit again. She decided to call the police. They were all too familiar with this man and were, like her, becoming rather tired of his nonsense.

Donna was told to write out a statement and the police were on their way. As she sat at the table, her daughter was on the internet. They had a huge front window, which left one quite visible from the front yard although they are surrounded by trees to lock them in. They heard three large bangs. Donna told her daughter to log off and call 911. Her daughter remained very calm and suggested they chase the perpetrator while bringing along their paintball guns. While very tempting, Donna refused to leave the house and insisted they stay inside. It turned out to be many eggs bashing against the window. She called the police again. They arrived shortly after the call.

The female officer and her partner were very familiar with Alan Harris. They were not going to let this incident pass. He would not get away this time. In the dark of the night with little light from the sky, they searched the forest surrounding her home. Donna joined them so she could point out trails leading to and from the property. Alan had befriended her wolf guard dog, so he could walk about the land freely. When they walked through the lower level where her car was parked in the carport, the officer noticed a letter on her windshield. How the hell did he do this? They had walked past the car three times. A black car under a bright light with a white letter on it. The letter would have been hard to miss! The police were surprised. They knew it was not there when they walked by earlier. Alan had been lurking on her property in the dark and this would become one of the charges placed against him.

This four-page letter was in Alan's handwriting, professing his love for her and clearly signed, I love you, Alan.

> . . . I said you'd never hear from me again, I lied, obviously. I have so much anger, sadness, fear, regret and not very much love . . . I have written this letter to find my positive feelings and to give you the love you deserve. As part of that process I am sharing with you my negative

feelings, which are holding me back. Just like my previous letter I don't care if you use this against me. I've done so much wrong. "Love is never having to ask!" I'm guessing that if you believe me, that I love you, that I will offer my support and you won't have to ask.

. . . I really love you so much. I do want to be your knight and I don't want to just agree with everything. I need to be me and I support you in being you. I love you. I want you to admire me. The next time when we talk I will be more patient and understanding. You do deserve that.

. . . P.S. "The response I would like to hear: I love you Alan, I really appreciate what a caring and understanding man you are. I trust we can work this out."

Oh brother she thought, as sad as it really was at the same time it was almost funny!

After an hour or so passed, the police left to arrest Alan. He was charged with Unlawful Entry, Harassment and Lurking on the Property at Night. She was subpoenaed to witness against Alan.

Over the course of the next eleven months the deals between Alan's lawyer and the Crown would change numerous times. At first there was an offer to relocate Alan. Then there was a Peace Bond offer and other agreements. Many people felt it was in everyone's best interest for Alan to relocate. His job was on the line and his choices were limited. Donna had faith that the system might actually be of some help this time. What would be his next move? How and when does this all end? Alan retracted his original offer to relocate. He was ready for trial and he wanted a fight. Donna was sure he counted on the fact that she had a fear of public speaking. He was well aware of the anxiety she suffered and chose to refer to it many times, as her weakness. Little did he know of her new found strength! She had major support. She was in total control of herself but best of all, she had her spirit back! Donna was very prepared for the trial.

YOU NEVER KNOW HOW
STRONG
YOU ARE...
UNTIL BEING STRONG IS THE
ONLY CHOICE YOU HAVE.

The police had introduced her to a Special Tasks Officer. She was absolutely amazing in Donna's eyes. Donna met with her twice a week for some time and she directed her in many areas. Areas like; Where to look during the court session. How to sit. What to hold in her hand. Most of all she taught her how to combat Alan's icy stare, should she find herself faced with it. She also taught her some self-defense. Donna was ready!

Court was scheduled for 1:30pm. As she approached the courthouse a woman called her name from a distance.

"Donna, can I talk to you, please?" she asked.

"Sure, do I know you?" Donna asked.

"No but I want to thank you for having the guts to follow through with this. Allan has caused me a lot of grief" she said.

"Why didn't you do anything about it?" Donna asked?

"Why didn't you do something sooner?" she answered.

"Good point, I was scared shitless" Donna said

"Good luck, I hope you kick his ass!" as she walked away.

Donna sat in a private room along with her team of support. As she looked out the window she saw him walk by impeccably dressed, well groomed with his head held high and his lips pursed in a tight strain. Alan was ready to fight! So was she! It took his lawyer thirty five minutes of negotiating to get him to plead guilty to one of the three charges against him. He agreed to the harassment charge in exchange for the other two charges being stayed and a conditional discharge, which included a peace bond for one year, probation and treatment for alcohol abuse. Everyone agreed the trial would have been grueling and with the way the legal system works they would have worked hard to intimidate her.

Donna felt as though she was ready to take the stand, however the crown prosecutor and Alan's lawyer made the deal. She was simply a witness. The judge was tough. He came down hard on Alan saying that Alan "Owed her" for the living hell that he caused her family, friends and her. With every sentence, the judge spat out at him, Alan's head jutted higher in the air until it appeared to be cocked in an unnatural position. The judge angrily told Alan that had Donna not agreed, he would never let him get away with this. He asked if it had all been explained to her and for a moment Donna felt as though he was hinting that she should go ahead to trial as they had him where he belonged. It was confusing but she wanted it to end. Once again, in order to save his job . . . he went . . . *Unpunished*.

They were all happy to be leaving the courtroom. Two women came over to Donna as she was walking down the sidewalk. Unnerved Donna smiled at one that had made eye contact with her.

"We're so glad you stood up against Alan Harris. He's a bastard!" one woman said.

"Yeah he's a piece of shit and that's giving him too much credit! Way to go!" the other woman said.

"What? Are you girls kidding me? What's your story?" Donna asked shocked.

They confided their fears and the incidents they had experienced with Alan. They had heard about Donna as the city was small and she was fairly well known, with her business and all. Donna admitted to them that at one time she would have died for this man . . . but not *because* of this man. They all celebrated as it was finally over . . . again.

Alan was ordered to go to treatment and he chose a psychologist in another city to avoid anyone he seeing him. After the RCMP had finally convinced Donna how dangerous he really was, she decided to call Dr. Benning and discuss the situation. Of course the confidentiality act did not allow for patient information being discussed, so he chose to ask her questions. She answered them honestly and he seemed totally surprised. The conversation continued and he then told her that this was a completely different story than what he was hearing from his client. He said after hearing the situation as Donna had explained it, it gave him cause to believe that her life was in danger. Alan was brilliant and Dr. Benning was now much more aware of the truths. He thanked her for calling and she in return thanked him for his opinion. It was still beyond her comprehension to accept the fact that she was truly in a dangerous situation. It couldn't be. How did she get into this crazy place in life? She read about other women and couldn't understand why they were stuck in a situation like this. She thought she was fairly intelligent. What the hell?

Then two weeks later her lawyer called. Donna hesitantly answered and joked that she really wasn't home because he likely didn't have good news for her. He said he didn't even want to tell her but Alan Harris had re-appeared.

"Oh Geez, now what"? she asked.

"He came storming into my office and tried to serve me on your behalf. I told him this was not a proper serve and that I wasn't representing you at this time, but he insisted on leaving the inch thick document in my office. Its absolute trash and totally insane. Donna this is a MOVIE!" her lawyer told her.

It was after the criminal court date that Alan went immediately up to the courthouse and filed a civil suit against her. He was representing himself and had been in the courthouse daily for many months preparing. He had started his plan of attack nearly eight months earlier. When does it end? When will he stop?

A good friend of Donna's who was an affluent lawyer in town, offered to represent her. He could not believe what was actually taking place. He was appalled to see what this was doing to her once again. He recommended that Donna not attend court that day.

Alan had written a signed affidavit, which was false, sick and demeaning. They told her it was all irrelevant. The only argument he had and a weak one at that was that he was demanding monetary compensation in the amount of $30,000.00.

Alan did a fairly good job at attempting law; however he upset the judge with his opening statement. When the judge repeatedly asked him what he really wanted from this woman; his answer always went back to, monetary compensation. The judge told him it was not going to happen. They bantered back and forth, and the judge tired and impatient, adjourned everything until July. He warned Alan that if he didn't stop, it was going to cost him. He repeatedly showed Alan the signed legal agreement in which they had already settled. Donna asked for nothing.

Donna's lawyer had told her there was a man in court who seemed quite interested in the case. Why was he there?

Time went on as she waited for July, some nine months down the road and once again into another year.

The rest of the year was not without incident. Donna was given pepper spray for her own protection. She was asleep one night, and was awakened by the sense that someone was watching her. She awoke with a start only to find Alan walking into her bedroom. She grabbed the pepper spray from under her pillow and let him have it!!

He screamed, "You fuckin bitch! You crazy fuckin bitch" and ran out.

How did he manage to keep getting in? A mystery the police could never figure out.

She became very strong emotionally, almost cold and numb inside. She vowed to remain cautious for the rest of her life.

She remembered a quote from her mother:

"I know sometimes you think I'm a cold, hard bitch, but when you experience some things in life it makes you tough"

And then she reminds herself . . . *Winners never quit and Quitters never win!*

Chapter 27

*M*onths later, a client recommended an internet site which seemed quite harmless. She was having a great time meeting people and felt it was no threat. Donna had previously explored sites and discussion forums on Religion, Divorce & Single Parenting. Now she was venturing into the unknown. A place where all walks of life could hide and disguise themselves and get lost in the unknown world of cyberspace.

How exciting could this be? There were people online from all over including many locals from their city. Donna had decided never to meet anyone but at the same time had hoped to make new cyber friends. That seemed safe enough. If she never went anywhere, she could lose herself in the online world. She found it rather amusing and frightening at the same time that people would actually post their pictures online. Some were business people in the community which were very well known.

Many months later after feeling quite comfortable, Donna decided to have some fun. Her impish side was returning. She had befriended a few people who were rather cautious about divulging too much information and she took it as a personal challenge to crack their codes. One man, who was as curious as her, would not divulge much about himself as he was a high profile business man in town. They had both shared the fact that they would be at a few local locations throughout the weekend. She was out for cocktails with a few girlfriends and it was apparent that they would be in the same establishment. They had exchanged cell numbers since at that time there was no call trace or way of finding a person.

Donna found it extremely funny to watch a man walking around looking for someone he had befriended, not knowing if she were brunette or blonde. Tall or short. Large or small. It was even more amusing to see him on his cell phone as she had hers on vibrate. As she was in the hallway, exiting the washroom, her daughter called. She was almost caught! He passed by her with a bewildered look on his face, as if wondering . . . . is that her?

Another night Donna walked into their local casino. Something she had never done, not to mention alone. But she had a new found strength. She would not panic or be weak! As she was walking with her head turned, in awe of all the noise, people and ruckus, she walked right smack into the man wearing a black leather jacket. As her face turned various shades of color, she apologized profusely. The man simply stared at her with dark brown eyes and a serious expression. He kept staring at her.

"Wow" . . . "Oh Wow" he kept repeating as if he had hit the jackpot.

She continued on her way to a private gambling room where the betting was only a nickel, since she was hardly a seasoned gambler. She thought to herself "I recognize this man." At least she thought she did.

The man decided to follow her to the room where he took a seat beside her. He started a conversation and was very easy to talk to. He had a great sense of humor and she found him pleasant enough.

Although giving him her phone number was out of the question, she did give him her email so he could contact her.

The first email was quite flattering:

> *Hi Donna, Thank you for this evening, I'm still reeling at your beauty, I honestly didn't expect to meet anyone with your looks and personality, so I'm well WOWED over it all. I hope everything was alright when you got home. I nearly crashed into the light post leaving the place, I have to tell you that you had my heart racing from the second I saw you. I hope we can get together soon, I'll be back from Regina on Saturday so if you're willing and have some free time, make a plan for us if you wish, I'm game for anything, I loved your company, even just sitting there looking at you was great!! Talk to you on email, enjoy your days off, you deserve it.*
>
> *Mervin*

Merv emailed her frequently, exchanging life stories and comparing common ground. He was newly separated. He was very much into the Catholic faith. So huge in fact that he attended church twice a week and went to confession one to two times a week as well. Hmmmm quite the Christian she recalled thinking. He must be a real good man.

Once she became comfortable with the man's history (as he told it) she agreed to a few visits. Merv was NOT a handsome man in her eyes. However some of his morals and opinions made him become attractive. This was always her theory in life. Some of the most physically beautiful people were the ugliest souls. Life was indeed interesting.

The more she got to know Merv, the more challenging and complex he became. She always enjoyed trying to figure people out, or so she thought.

In the midst of a nasty divorce, Merv told her he was accused of burning his family home down where his wife and children resided.

He was living in a trailer inside a quonset since his business was on the property. Interesting indeed! They both had recent fires. Donna's was in her business, his, in his home. He had also told her he was accused of internet porn among many other ills. Yes people get nasty in divorce as we all know.

It was August and Donna was attending her friends Rita and Kurt's wedding. She hadn't invited anyone to escort her. She was enjoying the outdoor function and the beautiful misty sunny day when her cell rang. Merv was across the road in the park. He had asked for a minute of her time. She walked across the road to find him in a jovial mood. There was no apparent reason for his call other than to enjoy her company. She stayed a little while and went back to the party.

In the beginning of their friendship Donna had introduced him jokingly as her bodyguard. She had confided in Merv most the gory details of her relationship with Alan. She explained that her reason for not wanting to get into another romantic relationship was because everything was still too fresh. She needed time.

Merv and Donna developed a close relationship. For six months there was the new romance and best behavior on both their parts. They had great conversations and fun times. At times he would seem to be fighting a dark demon. He would shut himself away and not answer calls. When he did, he seemed very depressed. So depressed at times, Donna feared he may take his own life. She went to his trailer in the quonset after one conversation where it was obvious he had been crying and was in a horrible state. When he finally answered the door he was shirtless and holding a slingshot and a rock. He was in fear of . . . something. Someone? His place was a disaster and reeked of tobacco. Beer cans covered the table, and it appeared he had not bathed in days. She spent a long time trying to console him. It seemed like a lost cause. Merv was very jovial some days, but that could quickly change to one of major sadness. Any slight comment would change his demeanor.

Over time, she met Merv's family. He had wonderful, God-fearing folks. A gentle, kind, soft-spoken mother and a father with gentle tones to his voice. He also had five sisters and a brother who were the most loving, closest, kindest people she had met in her life. Merv had good genes. Or so she thought.

As time went on, they became a couple. Although they always seemed to have their challenges as many couples do. In his depressive states he would want to be alone. In his happy moods, he wanted her. Donna persevered through many incidents which made her question him. Questions that when she asked, were always cautiously and smartly answered.

When one of his sisters told Donna in confidence that she should "move on" and that she "could do better", it made her think. Later, another sister told her the same thing. What do they know that she doesn't? Why would these lovely women say that about their own brother? What are they really referring to? Why won't they give me a clear explanation, she wondered.

Merv moved into an apartment in the city and he seemed to be sinking back into darkness. When she would visit there, she found it odd that he locked his bedroom door. He always appeared on edge if they were at his apartment. On the other hand he seemed quite content and relaxed when they were at her home. When leaving his apartment one day Donna ran into an old acquaintance in the hallway. They chatted briefly and Donna told her that her friend lived in the block

"You mean him?" she asked as she pointed to the closed door.

"Yes." Donna said.

"Oh wow." she said.

Donna left shortly after wondering what that comment meant.

Merv struck up friendships with many of Donna's friends. Most of them quite enjoyed his humor and his company. Her friend Pauline never quite felt comfortable along with a few others. They couldn't pinpoint it but something was "off". He was quite capable at making a good first impression. He was always offering his help with any tasks. She never really met any of his friends. He seemed to have left a life behind.

There was a woman connected to a provincial group he belonged to. Once, Donna and Merv travelled to Saskatoon to meet this woman and one of her friends. Donna was horrified to discover that he had planned for her to stay in a hotel room while he stayed with the other woman. She could not understand why he would do this. It turned into an argument she was not going to lose. Later she wondered why she bothered.

With both of them enjoying the same hobby, growing plants, fishing and being outdoors, they did have some memorable times. He did not like the fact at all that Donna would head out fishing alone. At one time while she was camping he sent out a friend to check on her. Very caring . . . or so she thought. The friend mentioned how worried Merv was about the bears in their forest where she frequently fished. She was never concerned about bears. The friend suggested perhaps Merv was concerned about two legged bears. They both laughed it off.

One of the gifts Merv gave her was a beautiful solid crystal heart ornament. It contained a smaller red heart held within a larger one. It truly was a beautiful gift. Apparently its meaning was that she was stealing his heart. She placed the heart on a table near the entrance to her home for all to admire.

Donna always missed attending church and had started to attend with Merv. She felt awkward as she was attending with a man who was still technically married. She struggled with this, and eventually she quit attending. Merv continued going and continued to have extra meetings with the Catholic Priest. She never questioned him having all these meetings since she simply chose to believe he was a good Christian man.

Chapter 28

They decided to take a trip to an island off of Cuba. The sun, sand, food and people were wonderful. They truly had a great time in the tropics. They decided to go snorkeling even though Merv was not a swimmer. Donna found it very odd that no matter how hard she tried to teach him to float . . . he simply could not. She always thought that everyone floated on the salt waters, not so for Merv. He couldn't swim well at all. The warm blue ocean water was beckoning to him to explore and he ventured further out. She watched as Merv drifted further out and she could only see his head every so often as the waves flowed over him

Suddenly Donna had a very uncomfortable feeling, even though she had snorkeled many times in many different tropical locations. She decided to stay closer to shore. She continued to snorkel along the shore but kept stopping and looking out at Merv.

"Help . . . Help" a weak voice cried.

"Merv?" she yelled.

She was helpless. Donna was not a strong swimmer and he was too far out. She yelled and pointed and two other groups heard her. One man was on a kayak and a couple on a paddle boat. Both of them headed quickly towards him. They arrived at the same time and pulled him aboard the paddle boat. By the time they brought him to shore he was foaming at the sides of his mouth and was totally exhausted. It was then, that the life guards arrived and checked him over suggesting that he had taken in too much salt water and wanted him to see the doctor. Merv weakly refused. They had a quad there and wanted to drive him back to the hotel room. He refused that as well. He chose instead to lean on her shoulder and slowly walk back to their room.

Merv spent the rest of the day in bed. Donna stayed on the balcony and checked on him frequently. The memory of years ago popped into her mind. She was at the lake with her mom and dad. As usual there was a lot of alcohol around and the men were whooping it up pretty good. One of them decided it was time for a boat ride. Donna was eager to go along with her dad. They all piled into the aluminum boat and paddled out in the water. Everyone was laughing and having quite the party in the boat. The rocking started and soon the boat was flipped right over. She was caught under the boat in the air pocket watching all the men kicking with all their might to stay above water. She could see her dad's paisley shorts under the water as he kicked his legged frantically. He couldn't swim. None of the men could swim. She was a bit of a water baby and decided to go up beside her dad. The frantic kicking forced her back under the boat. She tried to go up the other side. She awoke on the sand with her dad staring down at her with a terrified look as her mother was screaming and crying. She never forgot the look on his face and felt so sorry for him.

The maids stopped by often to ask if Merv would see a doctor. He refused. The next day Merv insisted that she never tell anybody about the incident . . . she thought it might be a lesson learned to share. Why did it have to be such a secret? Nevertheless . . . she never discussed it with anyone.

They returned home to Canada.

There seemed to be a dark side to this man, a cloak of darkness that seemed to envelope him, a constant battle from within. It was as though some type of demon haunted him. He openly shared that he was struggling with many things. None of which he shared in detail with her. He would hint that he suffered internally but it was not clear to her at this point why or what the cause was. It seemed that he was trying to warn her to stay away. Then at other times the message was completely different.

Over time the relationship became very strained. Donna was visiting at his apartment when she noticed his bedroom door was open. She noticed the beautiful crystal heart on his dresser. Was that her heart? The one he had gifted to her? When she got home she noticed the heart was no longer on the side table. It was a few days later when she questioned him about this, and he admitted that he had taken it back. She was shocked! He had expressed that she hurt his heart, so he saw it fitting that he take it back. She was at a loss for words and couldn't believe her ears. Who gives a gift and then takes it back without any mention?

The heart re-appeared and disappeared many times on her side table during the course of their relationship. Finally she had enough. On one of the occasions that she had the heart back in her possession, she took it out to the garage and shattered it with a hammer. Many weeks later, when she was riding in Merv's truck, she found the bag of shattered heart crystals sitting on the floor of his truck. She couldn't believe it! Why would he carry around this bag of shattered crystals? When did he take it from the garbage?

She would continue to receive emails with mixed messages-

Donna

I'm so fucked up over this. It's wed night, I'm pissed to the gills, my sister's gone back to Calgary, Dads not taking this well and I miss the hell out of you and if anyone can do everything wrong I'm living proof, I hope you're well and I'm glad you don't have to see me like this. All my Love

Mervin

For a while after he seemed to pull out of his depression and their relationship continued. His mother was ill and it didn't make life any easier for him. Then the darkness would take hold again and Donna would sense strangeness in him. It was as though there was a hidden personality. Merv would change his demeanor as well as his laughter. She felt a strong discomfort, but she could not put a finger on why. At intimate moments he would seem . . . . off.

After his reclusive states when he would return to some normalcy he would often try to talk to Rita. He would always make sure that her husband Kurt was never around. Rita felt uncomfortable with Merv. She would avoid private conversations. Kurt was quite intuitive and didn't enjoy the company of Merv.

There was a weird vibration type of sensation in Donna's bed that she could never explain when Merv stayed at her house. There had to be some reasonable explanation for it because it was simply her belief that everything can be explained. Or can it? Perhaps passing trucks on the road . . . . but there were none. There was no train that ran past her house either. Maybe it was her own nervous system or muscles playing tricks on her. She had mentioned it to Merv's father over dinner one evening, making a casual joke out of it. He also had no explanation but he did ask Donna's opinion. She told him she had no logical explanation. Even after she moved into a brand new home the vibrations continued.

She had the same old antique bed that she'd slept in for years. There were no trucks, trains or anything of the sort here. But there were definitely "vibrations" in her bed! She never believed in entities or other such phenomenon. All she knew was it was damn weird.

Merv fell once again in to his typical reclusive state . . . no contact. He would not answer his phone or return her calls. Then she would receive another email out of the blue—

Donna

*I know you're probably totally disgusted with me by now,
I do have some things to talk to you about, things about me
and why I'm so down on myself right now, not to keep you
guessing, but it has to do with sex. My feeling about this has
come to a head and I have to deal with it now. When I had a
break in Saskatoon yesterday I tried calling a therapist there,
but they have waiting lists a mile long. I can't believe that I
can't or haven't been able to talk to you about it, I've always
found it easy to talk to you about anything, but this one has
me tongue tied. This one is really embarrassing for me and I
don't know how to start the dialogue with you, or even if I
want to at this point before I talk to a therapist, I've put my
name on a waiting list. I'm packing a lunch and going for a
long walk today, I need time to think this through thoroughly
before I open my mouth about it. I hate making you suffer for
the way I am and don't know what else to do about it other
than the way I'm acting which I know you're not pleased with.
I hope I can tell you that I'm sorry and that you can accept it,
this all has nothing to do with you, adding to my problem is
what I know this is doing to you, I don't know which is killing
me worse, please be patient with me but if you can't I'll also
understand. I have to take my chances on everything right
now and face up to my issues that don't concern anyone but
me, but that I do know affect the people around me, especially
the person I love most, you!! I want to give you my all because
you deserve the best, right now I can't give you that.*

Merv

Well now, how was she to interpret that, she wondered? After
some time passed and he came out of darkness once again they
continued on. Now she was really curious as to who and what Merv
was really about?

D.D.K.

They had some fun times and many laughs. When he was on his high, he would find it difficult to be serious at all. Everything was a joke and at times Donna found it disturbing. She learned later that it also bothered some of her friends. Why can't there just be a happy medium, she wondered. The bright side wasn't to last very long.

Chapter 29

$\mathscr{M}$erv once again became more and more depressed. He was not happy in their city and was looking to start a new life somewhere else. He was offered a position in a family's business in the Cayman Islands. He had taken a builder's job in town for a while but he was not really happy. He had asked Donna her thoughts about this move, she totally supported it. She didn't think their relationship would be long term and realized that this would be best for him. It was obvious that she should have remained a friend and not have gotten romantically involved. They had discussed the move and she agreed that she would visit him on the island when she could.

It was right after Hurricane Ivan and the island was a destructive mess. Merv was renting a condo and the damage appeared to be minimal in this building. He wanted her to be comfortable on her visit so he neglected to mention some things. Then one evening when a friend was over the conversation came up about disturbing sleeps. Merv tried to quiet the man however he continued on. He spoke of when Merv was sleeping upstairs in this nice condo how something had run across him in bed. Merv tried to make light of it as though perhaps it was a mouse. In reality the condo was full of rats! They had reproduced at a rapid rate after the hurricane. Donna was no longer comfortable but persevered during the rest of her visit. Merv had told her that the couch was placed outside because of water damage from the hurricane. In fact it was infested with rats.

Donna decided to go for a day of snorkeling. After this horrible hurricane, the ocean bottom was on the sand, and the homes and contents lay on the bottom of the sea. What an eerie feeling to be on the top of the water and look down at personal belongings. To see a photo of a family lying intact far below was very disturbing. She cut the excursion short. They had no lawn chairs as everything on the island was scarce these days. Friends had offered theirs if she could retrieve them from their pool. Donna took a pole and managed to lift out two chairs amongst the fish that had been relocated from the ocean during the storm. What a weird site. She pressure washed these precious items and they now had new chairs. This visit was truly a unique experience.

They hosted a wedding for a young Jamaican couple who had no family on the island. A few people had brought food with Donna to prepare the main meal. The young couple sat out on the couch but was quick to jump up when something was felt under the seat. It really was funny, only because it wasn't her. After the function Donna went back outside to clean the barbeque. When she opened the lid, there was a rat staring up at her. It was not too shy either. They were actually kind of cute. Norwegian rats are furry and resemble Guinea pigs. The roof rats however were a different story.

Donna was seldom left alone for any period of time. She enjoyed exploring but Merv preferred her not to go anywhere alone for fear of her being raped. He managed to acquire two bicycles obviously taken from an abandoned property. Locals took advantage of making a quick buck during the aftermath of the hurricane. She was happy to have the bike along with Merv's permission to go on a ride. She set out on her journey to "Hell." It was about a half hour short ride to the small town where everyone was greeted by the devil. He would ask "How the Hell are you? Where the hell are you from?" and end it with "Have a Helluva good day." The small tourist attraction was a fun little place to visit. Unlike the *other hell* which she would later endure.

For Christmas Donna had decided to paint something for Merv. He seemed to appreciate what she considered her feeble attempt at art. So she spent every night after work and every spare moment she could, painting two pieces for him. One of which she titled "Darkness" and the other "The Light". The first had a man in dark cold waters surrounded by crooked dark trees, standing nude facing the dark sky with his hands held up in prayer. The second had a man standing in pristine, calm, turquoise waters with vibrant palm trees surrounding him and an angel reaching down touching his head. It was not exactly clear why she painted these in the manner she did. Merv's two children were flying down with her to see their father for Christmas. Each child would carry one of the wrapped gifts through their long journey. Merv was elated when he opened them.

Donna made a few trips to the island and enjoyed the warmth and apparent stress-free life Merv was living. He seemed very happy and content as she had never seen him before. They discussed an option for her to work there and set up a home for her daughters and her in the future. The first few visits were pleasant enough with Merv introducing her to new friends around the island. She would fly home to be with her daughters and then return months later.

Merv suggested Donna take a job on the island with people he had met from the United States. He was now renting one of their properties on the ocean in an affluent area. She could be a Vacation Property Manager which would allow her to go back and forth until her daughters were able to come. He would arrange an interview soon. Donna had to get a police record and a personal history file. She applied and received everything and gave all the paperwork to Merv on one of his visits home.

Donna was called by the couple in Texas and had agreed to fly out the next day to meet them. She was met at the airport and driven to their loft in the center of Dallas. They were very nice people and she was thrilled at the whole idea. The properties were just down the road from Merv's house on the highest point of the island. The homes were beautiful and they referred to them as the "mansions." They were tastefully decorated with unique full length wax statues situated in appropriate places. One was a pirate captain which was very life like. It amused her how the figures surprised the house guests as they walked up the stairwell and entered the dormer room. There definitely was an interesting item in each of the rooms. It took her many days to figure out one light switch. The maids were at a loss as well. It turned out when she left the switch on; a chandelier was lowered from the second story to allow for easy cleaning. Amazing she thought.

On one of her visits, she noticed how Merv still stood with his back to the wall . . . wherever they went. He still seemed to have paranoia of sorts. Was the darkness going to rear its ugly head on this beautiful island paradise? She was always under Merv's guard and if she was left alone it was without any means of transportation. The homes were on a dead end road and the ocean edge was composed of lava rock. One could not walk barefoot like they could in the tourist area. There was only a few sand beaches close by where one could wade into the waters.

As Donna was finishing the supper dishes she came across a strange item in the utensil drawer. It looked similar to a small dumbbell. She was trying to figure it out or open one end of it when Merv abruptly grabbed it from her hand.

"That's Roy's" he said sharply!

"What is it?" she asked.

"I'm not quite sure. He forgot it when he was here." He answered

Quite the reaction she thought. She let it pass.

Donna learned how to sit by the endless pool during the day waiting for Merv to arrive home. In the beginning it was like a wonderful Caribbean vacation. With time it became, hot and boring. She could not collect any pay cheques as she was waiting for the police records to clear.

"Soon" Merv always assured her . . . . "Soon"

Donna would later learn Merv had not in fact submitted the papers. She would later stumble across them and much more one day as she was sorting a closet out of boredom. Wow, what surprises indeed.

Donna did enjoy the experience of managing the mansions since the people who rented them where in a class of their own. She would make sure the maids had everything in order and that the pools were immaculate. Since there weren't a lot of rentals after the hurricane the homes remained empty most of the time. A family from Texas was to arrive soon and Donna had received their grocery list. The island was limited for shopping with the majority of stores catering to tourists. The list that was sent included many bottles of soda pop, chips, and candy. Specifically *black* jujubes. Donna headed out for an exciting day of shopping to gather up the goods. She went to all three of the island grocery stores but could only find assorted jujubes. She bought them all which still left her short of the count. She bought out all the soda pop that was left in the stores from this week's shipment. When she arrived back to the mansion she neatly placed the groceries in the pantry.

The next day Donna greeted the family upon their arrival. Jake, his fiancé, Jake's twenty year old daughter and his baby granddaughter were the first to arrive. They were familiar with the mansion since they booked it every year. The daughter was very entertaining.

"Daddy, there's only mixed jujubes in the pantry and I asked for all black!" she whined.

"Well that's all they had in the store." he said.

"Well daddy there's no cherry cola either." she said

"So drink coke!" he replied.

"Well daddy you're gonna have to fly me home. I can't stay a week without cherry cola and black jujubes!" she insisted.

Oh boy, here we go Donna thought to herself. Is this kid serious? She certainly was.

Donna and Merv went to the tourist area to sunbathe on the sandy seven mile beach. It was Sunday and Merv's day off. Donna's cell rang shortly after they arrived.

"Donna there's a huge centipede in the garage and I can't get into my car!" cried Jake's fiancé.

"Step on it." Donna said.

"Ahhh I can't it's huge!" she screamed

"Well can you get a broom and sweep it out? I'm twenty minutes away." Donna said.

"No! Now please come and remove this ugly thing!" she demanded.

Donna headed back towards the mansion. When she arrived she found a three inch caterpillar. She picked it up and took it outside.

The next day when Donna went over to the mansion to make sure things were going good, Jake's fiancé ran over to her.

"Oh God, can you please take me away from here?" I'm going to lose my fucking mind. Daddy . . . Daddy . . . Daddy, is making me fucking crazy!" she said.

Donna burst into laughter. So this is how the elite live? No thanks, she thought to herself. She promised if need be that she would take the woman out for drinks to escape the craziness. The next day, daddy's girl was flown home in his Lear jet.

The next group from Alabama was expected to arrive the next day to occupy the second mansion. A grandmother who planned the trip for her huge family. Her list consisted mainly of seafood and snack items. Donna wondered what surprises lay in store for her with this family. The lady was as sweet as could be. The only extra that she asked for was more pillows and blankets for the kids that were sleeping all over the floor. This house was packed. Since the hurricane had hit, the satellite dish was not back in order and the family was set on watching the football game. Donna scrambled but managed to find a man to fix the dish and all was well. She headed out to find the pillows and was surprised to find that there were only four on the entire island.

The family was happy during their stay and never asked for anything else. When they left Donna was surprised to see that the fridge was so full of food. They must have eaten out a lot she thought. She gave the maids some of the food but ended up with a cupboard full of canned crab, a whole tuna, and a lot of other seafood. Since she was not one to waste she asked Merv if she could host a dinner party. They invited everyone they knew which totaled around thirty people. The drinks were unlimited as the family had also left a fully stocked bar behind. It was a pleasant evening and Donna was happy to have everyone. She always enjoyed large gatherings.

Merv did take her to the other side of the island on occasion where it was very quiet and the water was turquoise. When she asked to stop at a local spot he became very agitated but agreed.

"Don't talk to any of the blacks. They're dangerous" he said.

"Oh, Come on." She said

"They're not to be trusted! I'm telling you baby!" he said.

Well that was rather odd she thought. He works with them and is friends with them, so how can this be possible? When they entered the building Merv chose an end table where he could sit with his back to the wall and see the whole room. Donna ordered a snack and struck up a conversation with the owner, an elderly black woman. She was very pleasant and they had a nice visit. She invited them back.

"Well that was sure scary" Donna joked.

Merv did not reply. After a day on the quiet pristine beach they headed home. Merv decided that they would stop at a spot where he knew the owner. They had a few drinks and a pleasant conversation. The man was clearly gay and Donna found it rather surprising because Merv had always displayed such homophobic actions in the past. She had some friends who were also homosexual and Merv had displayed his disgust at the thought. Homosexuality was frowned upon on this island. So much so that they refused to allow a gay cruise ship to enter the port and it made worldwide headline news.

As the sun was setting and they were about to leave there was a group of people standing on the pier. A tattered raft was coming to shore. There were eight adults and three children on it. It had no edges and had a very small motor. The raft was full of bagged blankets and it seemed no other provisions. The police arrived and ordered them to turn around. Donna was shocked! It was sunset, the tide was rising and they were sending these people and the small children back into the ocean. How could this be possible? They were given water and headed back out. They held huge bright smiles and waved farewell. They were Cubans. Trying to start a new life and that dream was soon shattered.

"We have to do something!" Donna demanded.

"They try that all the time, they should know better by now" Merv said.

Donna had a hard time sleeping that night. Was there something more she could have done? She wondered.

On New Year's they walked along the beach at midnight to see the fireworks against the sky and above the ocean. Bursts of pink and green with louds thunders appeared one after another. They were breathtaking. There were many wonderful warm days and beautiful sunset nights. There were equally many disturbing nights. Nights where Merv would scream in his sleep, flailing his arms. Had the demons followed him to his island paradise?

"Ha-ha, they'll never figure it out, hah, Stupid Bitch . . . . electrical hahaha" he spewed as he tossed and turned.

This was not the first time Donna witnessed Merv's sleep talking. In her new home he began to talk more in his sleep, out loud and in some detail. When she mentioned it to him he simply asked what he had said. She told him just some laugher with a "she" here and there. They attempted to laugh it off but Donna felt he was clearly talking about a fire.

Each visit became more strained. It seemed to Donna that Merv was very cautious around her and always questioning her. On this trip she would arrive and her laptop was not working. Merv had offered to take it to a computer repair shop. Two days later he had brought it back to her.

By the time Donna got up each day Merv was long gone to work. She would check her emails and eagerly write to her daughters and friends. She hadn't really noticed how few emails she was now receiving. With the service on the island and the land line phone service being second to cell service, she had not really thought about it. The telephone seldom rang and her cell seldom worked. When a week later Donna finally reached her daughter, she was very upset that Donna wasn't answering her phone. Donna became equally as upset as she never received any calls. On the contrary, Merv always called and always got through. He had her convinced that this was how the island worked. Some days it did . . . . some days it did not . . .

One morning an email Donna opened had her very confused. One of her friends asked if they had done something to upset her. Another asked if the email she had sent was in fact meant for them. She had no recollection of any emails to either of them. There was nothing in her sent folder or in her trash folder. Donna never really understood what was happening.

The next morning she awoke much earlier than usual. As she watched from the bedroom door, Merv was eagerly writing on her laptop.

"Good Morning" Donna said in a sleepy tone.

He was very surprised when he turned around and quickly said "Oh, hi baby".

"What are you doing on my computer?" she asked.

"I'm reading your emails." He quickly replied without expression

It made no difference to her since she had nothing to hide. Little did Donna know there was a lot more going on. Merv had taken it upon himself to email everyone in her contact list. To most he simply wrote . . . "Fuck off and stay out of my life" or "I don't want to hear from you anymore"

She found out that her friend Beth used her husband's email address, Merv didn't realize this. So he also told her where to go.

And so it began the saga of on and off again. Donna found letters from a girl in Cuba. She was no older than 21 and Merv had flown there while Donna was back home in Canada. Donna read her Spanish letters thanking him for the purse and asking when the other items were going to be sent. She found pictures of them in a restaurant in intimate moments. She also found letters from a lady in the Ukraine. Donna supposed one "Uke" wasn't enough for him. It was painful at first but she soon realized they were not meant to be. She mustered up the courage to confront Merv about the photos.

"Merv I'd like to talk to you about something." she said. "I was cleaning the closet and I found some pictures of you and a young girl. They look pretty recent?"

"Come and sit by my laptop." he said.

He proceeded to open up files. He was totally silent. There they were photo after photo of Merv and his young Cuban girlfriend. First sitting at a dinner table in a restaurant, then embracing each other, and then passionately in a steamy kiss. Donna could not believe he was doing this. What was his purpose? Was this a turn on for him? She was so furious! Donna looked at him with a cocky smirk on his face and she lifted her hand and smacked his face as hard as she could. He smirked. Her hand burned. What an idiot she thought. How dare he?

Donna got up and went outside to gather her thoughts and regain her composure.

Merv appeared quietly. "Baby, it didn't mean anything, honest" he smartly said.

She was beside herself. Why was he doing this? But better to be hurt by the truth than comforted with a lie she thought to herself. She wasn't feeling as though the whole relationship was very healthy. When she was leaving the island she suggested they not be a couple but asked to remain friends.

Chapter 30

*D*onna was home for weeks when the knock on the door sounded. There was Merv. She was about to close the door when he placed his arm inside.

"Please baby, please. All I ask for is five minutes" he begged.

She agreed. He begged for another chance and had excuses for his every action. She agreed to go back to the island. That was a huge mistake.

Months later Donna once again ventured out for what would be her final trip. Her girlfriend Shar was coming to visit. How awesome that would be. Filling the days until her arrival, she basked in the sun and sat near the pool at the mansions which she was now managing. Merv would continue to receive the pay for this position.

Shar arrived and they headed out in the jeep to greet her at the airport. Donna was so excited to have a friend there to share this beautiful place with. At first Merv was jovial and friendly towards Shar. But behind closed doors he frequently referred to her as the "whore". He didn't want the two of them to go anywhere without him. They had no vehicle; he needed the jeep for work. He did allow them to have it for a few days to venture to a beach or to shop. Then the demons took hold and he became more and more demanding. He preferred them to stay at the house during the day. There was nothing nearby and there was nothing to do. Donna wanted her friend to have a great time and was disappointed in Merv's controlling ways.

Merv was in a high frame of mind one day and decided that he was going to take the women to a special place on the island. They were taken to a spot in the ocean, out of site from the mainland. There was a huge sand dune and Donna and Shar could wade in the crystal blue waters. There they were with many stingrays. It was an amazing experience as the stingrays swam around them. Donna was enveloped by a huge one which wrapped right around her. Shar began to scream as fear surrounded her. Donna calmly asked her to quit screaming. It was a spot where many went to bathe with the creatures. The girls spent some time in the water and then boarded the boat. What a unique experience and one which would always be remembered. Days later people were forbidden to go into the area as a swimmer had been stung by one of the creatures. They had a few nice days, another in which found them at the turtle farm. Donna had tasted turtle burgers along with turtle soup previous to this visit. She now vowed never to eat turtle again as she watched the babies with their mother's wading in the pools of water.

As they lay in bed one night talking about the day and their plans for the next, Merv suddenly turned to Donna and with a strong straight index finger started poking her in the forehead.

"Why do you have to have all the other men online?" he asked.

"What men?" she frightfully asked.

"You have a bunch of men in your fucking life Baby!" he said

He was out of control.

"If I were interested in any other men why would I be here? Think about it!" she demanded.

This angered him even more and then he hit her on the side of the face with a closed fist. She tried to get out of the bed but Merv over powered her. As he continued to hold her down Donna tried to scream for Shar but she had earplugs in, which she always used to help her sleep, as well as a body pillow that she packed in her bag for the trip. Donna would be very grateful for that pillow in the next few days.

Merv positioned himself on top of Donna as she tried to fight him off. He laughed mockingly.

"Oh Baby" he taunted.

Donna managed to knee him in the groin and that just fueled his fire. She never knew that pain was his pleasure! It fueled his sex drive like fuel to a plane. He got higher and higher from pain. She broke into a weak sob, begging.

"What do you want from me Merv?" she cried

"I want to be your bitch!" he snarled and growled in a sickening voice. "I want you to hurt me. Come on baby, hurt me"

Oh my God she thought to herself. How did I get here?

"Hit me!" he said

So she did.

"Harder" he demanded, "Scratch my back, make me bleed."

"I can't" she begged. "I just can't."

Merv's back was covered with boils and extreme acne. She had tried to help him get rid of it to no avail. It bothered her when he was shirtless. It was an extreme case.

It seemed like he was possessed. Donna managed to get out of the bedroom and ran to Shar's room. Shar was in a daze and thought she was dreaming at first.

"What's happening?" Shar asked half asleep.

Then Shar witnessed him hitting and dragging Donna by her hair. All the while Donna was trying to fight back. She fell to the floor and Merv grabbed her by her feet. As Shar begged him to stop, he continued to drag Donna by her feet across the cold tile floor. Then he picked her up and Donna grabbed a bar stool at the counter for relief. He lifted that stool and slammed it down on the top of her right foot. The pain was excruciating and as Donna was yelling and Shar was begging, he dragged Donna down the tile stairs by her hair and threw her out the door onto the gravel lot! She got up and ran and quickly hid behind the cement fence.

Now she needed to think of what to do next. If she ran to the mansions, he had the keys. If she took the road, he would find her. If she took the way through the trees she could not walk barefoot on the lava rock. Donna was trapped. Merv and Shar appeared out on the balcony. Donna could hear every word between them. Merv rambled on to Shar about all the men Donna was seeing. Shar tried to assure him there was no one. She was her close friend and she would know.

"She's lied to both of us!" he insisted.

He sounded very convincing. Shar kept her wits about her and simply listened.

"Please Merv, let her back inside. With the elements, scorpions, spiders I worry about her survival." she pleaded with him.

"She's a survivor" he numbly replied.

And so she was . . . Donna listened for the next few hours and when Shar went to sleep, Merv went on the hunt. Oh Lord, please don't let him walk behind this wall, she prayed. He drove off towards the mansions. It would take him some time she knew as there were two homes and they were very large. Donna could hide until he found her. She thought about where to go and what to do. She could see the jeep. She could feel the closeness of the lights. He was back.

He walked to the cliff edge and then back towards the house. Was he walking towards her? She tried to hold her breath. The door slammed. He was back inside. She could hear some talking and then he was back outside, the jeep was leaving again. Donna had no cell. If she could get her laptop she would be able to email for help. She waited until he was gone and ran as fast as she could up the stairs to the counter and grabbed her laptop.

Shar was visibly shaking. "Please stay?" she begged.

"I'm ok. I'm going to email someone for help. I promise I'm close to the house and I won't leave you alone" she said

Donna ran back outside and she could see the lights approaching. He was back again. She jumped around the wall. Quickly she lay down and hoped she was unseen. He stood outside. She could hear his breathing. He walked toward the house and went in. Her heart thumped. Her laptop was dead! She used it as a pillow as she slept on the gravel behind the cement fence. Her fear of spiders disappeared. Her breathing was calm. She watched a black beetle climb the wall with a clicking sound as it moved. She stared at the stars. What should she do next? If she could get to the mansion for a short while she knew there was a cable to a laptop. There was also a phone. She couldn't risk it. She prayed.

Merv came outside again. As soon as he drove out of the yard Donna ran to the house. Shar was beside herself only pretending to sleep. He was back! The door closed. Had he seen her? Did he know she was there? Shar quickly shoved her beneath her body pillow on the floor beside her mattress. She half lay on top of her. Both of their hearts were thumping. Donna could feel the beat of her heart.

Shar pretended to sleep. They didn't say a word. Merv was silent. He went to bed.

Morning arrived and it was time for him to go to work so he left. Shar and Donna realized that they needed to come up with a plan. Shar insisted she was not leaving the island without Donna. They needed to contact someone. Anyone!

Merv came back sooner than they expected . . . she was still in the house.

"Hi Baby" he cockily said, as though nothing were wrong. "Can I speak to you in the bedroom please"?

You have to be kidding me, she thought. The conversation was one of total denial on his part.

"I never hit you. You don't have any black eyes or broken bones." he said.

In fact she was very tanned and indeed bruised, from groin to knee and elbow to wrist. Her arm was sore and her cheek was sore but he was right, nothing was broken.

Chapter 31

They were invited out to dinner one evening and Merv wanted Donna to be a "good girl". Shar was anxious to go to the friends so she could ask for help. Donna was afraid to tell them because she knew Merv had filled them with untruths about her.

Dinner was very nice but Donna was clearly nervous and uncomfortable.

Come sit with me baby!" Merv said.

She did her best to stay away from him. As the women were clearing dishes, Shar told Ellen that she needed to talk with her. Donna sat silent as Shar told her story from behind a post which blocked her view to the men. Merv was slyly watching.

"Why didn't you call or come to our home?" Ellen asked Donna.

"We only have limited calling and there are restrictions placed on the cell that Merv gave me, when he allows me to use it." She said

Ellen appeared shocked. The rest of their conversation was interrupted by the men.

Donna kept thinking of Merv's words to her.

"Do you really think anyone is going to believe you? First there was Alan Harris and now me?"

Her head was reeling with these thoughts. How foolish she had been to share those journal entries about Alan Harris with him. Rita told her how obsessed Merv had been with her journal entries. He told Rita how awful Donna's past had been. He now admitted he was the man in court that day! He sat through the whole session and obviously remembered all the details. How was she going to get off of this island?

Two more nights and Shar would be leaving. They had to figure it out. Shar was adamant that she was not leaving without her. Donna was so very thankful for her loyalty. They left the dinner party and Merv never left her alone until morning when he went to work.

The next day Merv kept leaving and returning home unannounced. At the end of the day he raced his jeep straight for the cliff as if he were going over the edge. He stopped right on the edge, got out of the jeep and opened a beer. Shar and Donna were watching from the balcony.

"Hey baby, grab a glass of wine and come join me" he yelled out.

Not a chance in hell she thought! He beckoned to Shar to join him. To keep the peace for another day she did. Donna stayed inside and opted out of the "view". She watched from the window to make sure Shar was ok. Merv appeared irrational and on a high. Shar just went along with his banter, adding little to the conversation.

Shar admitted to Donna that she was terrified that they may end up at the bottom of the cliff. Donna's thoughts were exactly the same. Now that Donna knew some of Merv's deep dark secrets he would consider her a threat. He would constantly have a glass of wine or a drink ready for both Donna and Shar. They knew that he could use that against them if anything were to happen. They would cooperate with Merv's every request until they could get off of this island. Often one would dump their drink to avoid becoming drunk.

As Merv and Shar were outside Donna prepared for her escape. She went to get her passport to be sure she had it when she could get away. It was gone, along with her visa card and other credit cards. She had no identification! Now what was she going to do?

When Merv came into the house Donna asked "Where's my passport and I.D?"

"You don't really need them." He said.

"I would like them back." She said

She was under his control. He demanded what he wanted and in order to live to tell this story she gave in to his demands.

"You're so little" he whispered as she was doing what he asked of her. "You're so little baby" . . . . They made it through another night.

In the morning Merv left later than usual. When he did go, Donna found her passport. She thought about what to do with it, so she hid it in a coffee tin on some rocks by the ocean. She thought if anything happened to her, someone would eventually find it and wonder why it was in a tin can.

Donna and Shar were trying to come up with a plan. Shar was leaving tomorrow. They only had one more day. They tried the phone, it was working! They decided to call Merv's cousin's wife. Sara was a God-fearing woman and one of the few people Donna knew on the island. Donna told her a bit about what happened. She seemed very calm and Donna felt as though perhaps Sara didn't believe her.

"Can I speak to Shar?" Sara asked.

Shar had heard everything Donna told her. When Sara asked her what happened, Shar had elaborated, telling her far more than Donna did. Sara then asked to speak with Donna again.

"Do you think anything will change if you stay?" Sara asked.

"No I don't." Donna answered

"Do you want to leave?" she asked

"Yes I do want to leave!" she answered. This was truly enough!

Sara promised to pick her up at the house and she would help purchase a ticket. Donna could repay her when she returned home. Donna was elated and at the same time very afraid. What if Merv caught them? What was he capable of? There was no other option. She had her passport.

Donna also called her employee Sandra as she was booked to come visit them. Donna had planned to surprise her with a gift of travel since she thought Sandra was deserving of it at the time. Donna didn't know what to say but the sadness in her voice gave it all away.

"Did he hurt you" Sandra asked.

"Yes" she said.

"I'm not coming to the island." Sandra said.

"I'm trying to get home." Donna said

It took months of saving to purchase the ticket to the Cayman Islands. A dream of a lifetime she thought for sure. Sandra had never been on a plane and Donna was very excited for her.

Shar had asked Merv to buy her some beer. He obliged and would not let her pay for it. She left twenty dollars on the counter which he left untouched. Tomorrow is the day. Anxiety was setting in. Merv had told Donna there was no room for her in the jeep to see Shar off at the airport. Even though, the two of them had picked Shar up. She stayed silent. One more night . . . just one more night.

Donna's head was spinning all night. She was worried about everything. Is this going to work? Sleep . . . just sleep. Sara had told her to be ready. She would pick her up after Merv left to take Shar to the airport. Donna's heart was racing!

Sleep just sleep.

Chapter 32

Morning arrived. Today is the day! Donna had one suitcase which she had used for several flights over to the island. She had to pick only what she needed and leave the rest behind. She didn't care. Donna didn't need anything as far as she was concerned. It was worth leaving anything behind.

Merv told Shar he would be back in time to drive her as he went to work. In the meantime Shar helped Donna quickly stuff her suitcase and carry it downstairs to the garage which housed the laundry room. They hid it beside the dryer. Hoping and praying he would have no reason to go there.

It was time for Shar to go. Donna remained upstairs as they waited for Merv to arrive.

"Where's Donna?" he asked.

"We said their goodbyes" Shar said,

As they were approaching the end of their road Merv asked "Why are you shaking?"

"I'm afraid of flying". She said as her heart thumped.

"Let's have a drink before you leave for the main terminal." He Said.

"I just want to go through security and get that part over with." Shar said.

He kept on about having a drink but she managed to convince him otherwise. She feared that Donna would arrive at the same time.

As they were on the main highway, they passed Sara on her way to get Donna.

"I hope she's going to talk some sense into Donna." He muttered.

Shar stayed silent.

Sara arrived and Donna was ready! She dragged her oversized suitcase out of the laundry room and to the trunk of her car. Sara had to help her lift it. As they drove off, Donna never looked back. She would never return here again. She was shaking and very nervous.

"Why are you so nervous?" Sara calmly asked.

Hah she thought, are you kidding me? And she quietly sat thinking.

> *"Better to die fighting for freedom then be a prisoner all the days of your life."*
> —<u>Bob Marley</u>

But she dare not say anything for fear of not getting out of this mess. Donna didn't give her any sexual details because when she started to tell her, Sara stopped the conversation. Sara assured her that she was safe with her and that there were guards at the airport should any conflict arrive. It didn't make Donna feel any better. Until she was passed the security gate Donna would not feel safe.

They went to a travel agent to change her ticket. Donna was in fear that they may not be able to or there would be no seats. Her chest ached. All the paperwork was completed and Sara used her credit card to pay for the ticket. They were now on their way to the airport. As they were approaching the building Sara pulled over.

"I want you to do something." she said. "I want you to call Merv."

Oh my God Donna thought.

"Why?" she asked.

"I am concerned about his mental state and don't want him to go home to an empty house. After all he *is* family." Sara said

Whatever Sara wanted, Donna would oblige. It was her way out.

Sara called him and said "Hello Merv".

"Hi" he replied as though nothing was wrong. "Is Donna with you?" he asked.

"Yes she is Merv and she has told me some disturbing things." She continued on with the conversation.

"I am taking her to the airport so she can go home. I will hand her the phone."

"What are you doing, baby?" he asked.

"You hurt me and I am not going to tolerate your behavior. We are done!" Donna said.

179

He denied everything . . . Donna handed the phone back to Sara. He continued his denial.

"Shar has also told me what you did Mervin." Sara calmly said.

It was then he admitted that he pulled Donna across the floor. At that point it was validated between the three of them.

"She stole twenty dollars off the counter." Merv said

"Did you?" Sara asked.

"Yes but it was Shar's money." Donna said

Merv had taken any money Donna had and the twenty was all they had. Sara insisted Donna give it back. She did.

Donna thanked Sara for her help. She ran into the airport straight through security. She had no money, but she had her passport. As her heart pounded she went through security to find Shar standing waiting. When Donna saw her, they both cried and held each other. They didn't care who saw. They were free . . .

When they arrived at the Miami airport they realized they only had a few dollars. The security dogs were constantly sniffing at them. I'm sure it was due to the nervous scent they may have been emitting. They were hungry so they opted to share a piece of pizza and a beer. They talked about their fears on the island and how they couldn't believe this all really happened. What an insane experience! It was like a bad dream. They compared it to a scary movie they had both seen in the past. Now this was to become their past. As they went to check in their bags they were overweight. Neither of them had any money left to pay the fees so they juggled a few items in their suitcases and Shar decided to leave behind a book she was reading. The weight had allowed Shar's bags through without any more issues. Soon they would be back in Saskatchewan and it would all be behind them. All they had to do was get through the Canadian customs. Donna was the last in line and with her luck she was chosen for a complete inspection. Oh my Lord she wondered, what next? Her daughter was waiting on the other side of the gate. It was late and Donna was exhausted. She wondered if somehow Merv had reported her. But for what she thought? As the customs officer proceeded to go through her bag she felt as though she was going to have a complete meltdown. The customs officer even went through her lipstick. Donna was curious and asked her why she was doing this?

"It's just a regular security procedure" she said. "Sometimes people like to hide drugs in their cosmetics."

Oh brother Donna thought. Just get this over with. She finally walked through the gate to find her daughter waiting. Thank you God!

"Do you really want a nut like that back there?" the officer openly asked.

"Nope" she replied. Even if it meant he went . . . . un-punished.

Merv had sent her email threats:

> *I have live nude cam sessions that you sent to Billy wanna seeeee them????*

Wow . . . you have got to be kidding! Donna wondered how he was creating these. She never saw them. She did know that she never did any such thing. She was convinced he was totally evil.

Merv called her close friend Anne. He asked Anne and her husband to please hear him out. Anne was appalled by his vulgarity. She was an avid member of the same church that Merv attended. Anne said it was as though he was reading all of his words. She was in shock as was her husband. Anne had always been and remained to this day one of Donna's strongest links. It would be hard in life to find a lady as precious as this one.

Merv had emailed Donna's close friends in her social circle. He told them she had reported them to Revenue Canada, and she was about to report another couple who she was friends with. As two of them were already being audited as well as Donna, they questioned her loyalty. She was devastated that anyone of these people would question her however she knew how convincing Merv could be. She wondered why she being audited. There was an email to his sister which he forwarded to Donna to make sure she read it. It was long, nasty and extremely belittling. He mentioned looking forward to meeting a new lady from Costa Rica . . . .

> *She's the one I told you who owns a restaurant in Costa Rica and another in Belize; I'm looking forward to meeting her!!*

Donna found it interesting how he was accusing her of talking to men online and then he wrote this. He knew Costa Rica and Belize where on her wish list of places to travel.

Merv told his sister how all of Donna's friends were tired of her and how she lied to everyone. Donna had emailed his sister when she escaped off the island. She was trying to let someone know that there was a serious problem with Merv. When she read the forwarded email she couldn't believe the things he had wrote. His mind was sharp but his honesty was obsolete. He wanted Donna to feel disliked and he was winning this battle. She didn't know who to trust anymore. Then she reminded herself . . . *Don't expect everyone to understand your journey . . . Especially if they've never had to walk your path!*

He was cunning, sly and brilliant.

He emailed her lawyer who was also a dear friend of hers. Al and Donna had attended many functions together and a romance never blossomed but they always stayed close. She adored his family. Donna asked Al to send a letter to Merv asking him to stop contacting her clients, friends and family. Also to ask that Merv return the data which he had removed from her computer. Al called her when he received the reply.

"Donna, over the years my firm has received some disturbing emails and letters, this is by far the worst, sickest and most perverted ever!" he said.

He was very upset.

"I do not want you to read it. It's obvious that Merv spent a lot of time constructing the letter." Al said.

"Send it to me Al, I want to read it." she insisted

It displayed how articulate Merv really was. It was awful:

Hello Al.

Without Prejudice

Concerning the letter your letter of March 24th representing Donna Campbell.

I'd first like to comment on her dramatized accusation of physical abuse, Donna should realize that not everyone will put up with her childish tantrums and yes she was escorted accordingly and within the law out of a house and no more or less force than necessary was used!! Her disappointment in herself for her actions and of losing out on some very lucrative salaries and life in the Caymans is no excuse for her behavior!! Her only injury was her self-defeating dysfunctional pride!! If a civil court case here in the Caymans is what she wants, there are enough people here that will testify against her foolish accusations and also these are people that she think she may have considered friends or allies. Most all people who are around d for any length of time quickly develop a sixth sense for her dysfunctional dramatized bullshit, I think this is just a simple case of Donna having sour grapes for being sent home like a child because she was caught whoring herself on-line with single men once again. She's not to be trusted as a Friend, especially as a partner nor would I expend much energy on her as a client who first of all lies and dramatizes alot and secondly cannot afford to pay attention never mind the cost of having you send such a senseless and petty letter like this!! To let it be known she did tell me about you and not in a flattering manner, her judgment against you was that you were equivalent to kissing like a toilet, I'm not sure what that quite means but take it from me D has no respect for anyone especially people like you or I that have treated her well. She's not worth the skin she lives in; she's a scammer and a user of any man who will do the littlest thing for her!

As far as her definition of friends go, her daughters included, they are also my friends and we have been in mutual contact and still are, and probably always will be, so she needs to comes to terms with that and get used to the idea!! Whatever I discuss with them is between them and I. Perhaps if she spent less time and money chasing around with men that she meets on the Internet like an old female dog in heat, she would be able to pay her bills and have a clearer conscious!! So, Al the only detriment to her reputation and business is not caused by me but is self inflicted by D herself, it's a pattern her life she has followed and is now catching up with her!! She was under the influence of alcohol at the time that she told me about her friends and Revenue Canada, so perhaps as her friend and council nudging her into AA's would be good advice for her!!

I have not had contact with her for months so again she's probably just mad and very humiliated like always at herself, and is using you to vent some frustrations towards me because I will not answer her emails anymore. I'm sure once again in her life, like countless times before she's humiliated herself with her actions pertaining to men, and now, as in the past has a need to blame her faults, shortcomings and dysfunctional life on someone else. Face it Al, have you ever met a woman who bleeds of victimization like her, it's not always the man's fault that relationships fails, but easy for a scammer like her to make people like you and a lot of other people believe her "She'll use and fuck the next guy up just like she did to me".

To answer to your letter:

1) I have none of her data

2) I am not tampering with her emails nor have I ever!!

3) I have no desire to send her any emails and haven't for months. In fact she's the one who emailed me last and when I read the pshycotic undertones of the letter I did not reply her and have no intentions to, perhaps she's once again heartbroken, angry, disappointed and distressed that I want nothing to do with her now or ever!! Women like her are a dime a dozen on the streets of any city of any country and for less than a dime one could do much much better than D.

She needs to stop trying to flatter herself, she's past middle age in her life and her emotional state is leaning over psyhcitso, her physical is pretty much esthetically gone, so she should seek professional Psychiatric help to try and work out her emotional problems that have plagued her from birth and her dysfunctional life of physical, alcoholic and sexual abuse that her many different fathers and mother have left her with, perhaps being raped by her third father at age 15 is now surfacing in her life!! Just a guess!! D thinks she can coast through life with a pretty face but she'll one day figure out that dignity, respect, honesty, sincerity and a bit of fidelity would go a lot further!

In closing Al, please use your better judgment on this, you are a professional and although I know you are Friends with D I think they both know that this letter is a joke, the justice system in Canada and in the Cayman's has little time to deal with real issues, never mind the pettiness and dysfunction of a jealous women's rage and revenge who's self sabotaged another relationship!!

I hope that as you have CC your letter to D that you also show her this one, she needs to deal with her losses; it's not her first and won't be her last!! D like her mother is every man's and any man's whore who'll pay her an ounce of attention or spend money on her, and I'm sure living in the same city you'll witness her go through many more bad relationships till she's so decrepit like her mother that she'll just settle. She really is a pathetic whore and a bad excuse for women; quit being fooled by her victim stories.

Sincerely and Without Prejudice
Merv Galloway

Merv had also sent her copies to both of her email addresses so he was sure she would read it.

Wow! How many people and who had been contacted. It took years to learn of more. Just when you think it can't get any worse, it can. And just when you think it can't get any better, it can.

Donna is calmed at the thought of a quote:

"Who are you to judge the life I live?
I know I'm not perfect
-and I don't live to be-
but before you start pointing fingers . . .
make sure your hands are clean!"
—*Bob Marley*

Donna was told Merv was coming home for a visit. She made sure she was unavailable. She had left her boler camper on a friend's acreage. Merv had joined her friends up at the lake, likely thinking she would be there. They told Donna when they woke up after a good night's bash that Merv was gone. No one could agree on the time but they all did agree he had left. The friends whose home Donna had left her boler at called to tell her that her boler had been vandalized. The tires had been slashed and her slicker coat which she always wore fishing had been taken. The TV and small change had been left behind while her personal ID and registration had been scattered throughout. Ironically a neighbor had witnessed a noisy truck circling the property and stopping on the road. Merv owned a diesel truck. Donna later received an email from him with her full legal names in it. Few people knew her birth name in full. The RCMP was called in but there were no prints as it had rained and Merv had left the country once again . . . . un-punished.

It was during this visit that his ex-wife's home had another fire. His children and wife were in the city at the time . . . . coincidence?

As she was reading the Island news one day and clicking on additional links . . . . there he was,

Men Seeking Women in the Cayman Islands

44 year old Man
Looking for Women
Living in Georgetown,
Cayman Islands

44 year old Man, Living in
Georgetown, Cayman Islands

Gender: Man
Birthdate: May 31, 1961
(44 years old)

Lives in: Georgetown,
Cayman Islands
Occupation: Production
Manager

Profile for Angelfinder2

I am a loving, kind, gentle, caring, honest, high energy, responsible man who loves life and all that it has to offer. I believe in live and let live! I am a Canadian born and have just moved to the Cayman Islands in the last six months. I am actively seeking my life partner!!

Interests: Animals,
Dancing,
Entertainment,
Exercise
and Fitness,
Fine Dining,
Gardening,
Healthy Living,
investment Real
Estate, Music,
Nature/Ecology,
Travel

All of the while Merv was dating Donna; he was actively meeting other women. Did the others on the island know? Was she that naïve? How humiliated she was. "Well of course she thought" . . . Donna had recognized him that night in the casino when they first met. He was on the dating site that was first recommended to her by friends. She had chosen not to reply to this man.

As Merv was chatting online with Donna from Ellen's house, professing his undying love once again . . . . she quickly sent the whole dating page on screen for everyone to see. She finally had proof.

"Tell the truth, or someone will tell it for you." She said out loud.

Oh but he would soon doctor that as well. He sent her another email, falsely written as though she was making it up and trying to get even. He was truly brilliant. When Donna read the emails herself she couldn't believe how well he had done creating them. Desperate measures were taken by Merv as he attempted to get her to come back one month later, as seen by the following email:

> *"Donna I had one of my men killed in an accident yesterday and Ritchie was involved and is in the hospital in shock and under heavy sedation, I could really use your support and your ear right now, please call me or email me!! Please!"*
>
>

Ton Homme
Merv

"Are you kidding me," she thought with a flustered mind. After all the trash emails and calls to her friends was he actually going to try to make contact again? You have got to be kidding! Was he ever going to stop?

Donna reminds herself a quote by Robert Frost: "*In three words I can sum up everything I've learned about life: it goes on.*"

She always said "*It's called Life, this journey we are on. So play the best hand you can, with the cards you are dealt. There's no winner. Just stay in the game and be the best you can. Quitters never win and winners never quit.*"

Chapter 33

Donna received the call from her friend Tanis. "Have you heard"? She anxiously asked.

"Heard what?" Donna asked.

"Merv was killed on the island" Tanis said.

Donna felt anger. She did not feel sadness. It was true. Donna found the online newspaper article:

> **"Cayman police confirm Sask. man was victim of homicide"**
>
> **"An autopsy has confirmed that a former Saskatchewan man found dead in his seaside rental home in the Cayman Islands was the victim of murder. The Royal Cayman Islands Police Service said Thursday that Mervin Galloway, 47, suffered multiple injuries to his head and body caused by sharp and blunt objects.**

"The post-mortem shows that Mr. Galloway suffered very serious injuries, which could only be caused by another person or persons," said Det. Insp. Kim Evans. And no one has been charged in his death. Galloway, a former resident of Saskatchewan (Canada) who had been living in the Cayman Islands for the last four years, was last heard from in the city of Bodden Town on Sunday. His body was discovered by a co-worker, police said there were no signs of forced entry at Galloway's residence."

Like many others Donna wanted to know who and why? She had her own suspicions. Was this a sex crime? She had long since learned that Merv had many "different" preferences. Had this been too much for someone? Drugs? Her mind was in turmoil. It appeared, according to the news that he was dragged, or fought his way, down the same stairs that he had dragged her down.

"Mr. Galloway's body was found on the ground floor of the dwelling house, lying in a pool of blood in a fetal position. He was wearing blue jean pants and a

black open-arm T-shirt all covered in blood. The body appeared to bear multiple blunt trauma about the head, chest and arms, including skull fracture, puncture wounds to the scalp and stab wounds to the scalp, arm, left flank and buttocks."

There were no answers to be found. She could only hope that the police investigations would be able to provide some. She discovered from reading the news articles concerning his death, that she was not the only woman he had been involved with, in fact, there were indeed many girlfriends—some even during the time they were together. Her suspicions had been confirmed . . .

> **"Before his death in May 2008, Mervin Galloway was a strong, affable man who lived alone but had several girlfriends; his cousin told the court on Thursday. Asked if he had any girlfriends, Mr. Allan said there were a number of women Mervin went to lunch with or dinner or went out with. 'I can only imagine he had some stay at his house now and again,' he added."**

> **"He said there was one woman Mervin was courting. He knew Mervin had sent her flowers. Mr. Akii asked if he knew whether the woman had a boyfriend at that stage. Mr. Allan said he did not know at the time, but he heard it later."**

Perhaps a jealous boyfriend has exacted their revenge.

Sometime later a twenty eight year old man was arrested and brought to trial for Merv's murder. It was during the trial that more questions were raised about Merv's death. However, no clear cut answers were ever found. Even the jury could not decide if this young man was guilty. The prosecution however tried twice more for a conviction, but was met with the same result. Not enough evidence to determine by a reasonable doubt that this young man was guilty. As of the writing of this book, no one has been charged with Mervin Galloway's death.

Donna accepted the fact that people do horrible things. She realized that we cannot undo all the wrongs in life. We all make many mistakes during our time on earth. She continues to ask forgiveness for her own mistakes. She still believes we are all on a journey and that we are taught many lessons. She also believes that when we pass a lesson, we are given another. Donna's belief is that we are never given more than we can handle. When times are tough, remember to just get through today. Tomorrow always brings a new day. She likes to remember as Papa always said *"If life gives you lemons, add vodka."* It's her sincere hope that people think about their actions and take responsibility for them. She truly believes that if we make amends and ask for forgiveness that we will be given a clearer conscience, contentment in our hearts and a strong sense of becoming the best person we can be. *Always stay true to yourself because there are very few people who will always be true to you.*

More questions kept coming but no answers followed. Would Donna ever find out what happened the night of Merv's death? That question still remains.

What a mix of emotions she felt! Mostly she felt angry. Angry that Merv didn't live long enough, to tell the truth, to be remorseful about everything that he said and did. Not only to herself but to the other people that had been a part of his life. The things you do for yourself are gone when you are gone, but the things you do to and for others remain as your legacy. She was angry that he left everything . . . unanswered. She also felt pity besides the anger and sorry for Merv and others that are so stuck in "the darkness" and cannot seem to get out of it. How awful to be in such an ugly place.

She wonders, was he indeed . . . . Unpunished?

Conclusion

As Donna sits on the deck, sipping her coffee, she ponders over how wonderful her life has become over the last five years since Merv's death. She has met and become engaged to a wonderful man, Richard Jenkins, moved to Eden and opened a restaurant. She has a closer and more loving relationship with her daughters and has two fantastic grand-daughters. She has overcome many obstacles on her path of life but these have only managed to make her a better and stronger person. She smiles warmly as Richard approaches. As he leans down and pecks her cheek, she thinks to herself, "I can hardly wait to see what life has in store for me now, I know it can only get better from here!"